Cybersecurity

An Essential Guide to Computer and Cyber Security for Beginners, Including Ethical Hacking, Risk Assessment, Social Engineering, Attack and Defense Strategies, and Cyberwarfare

Contents

Introduction

You have just found out there's such a thing as cybersecurity. Do you create tons of accounts you will never again visit? Do you get annoyed thinking up new passwords, so you just use the same one across all your accounts? Does your password contain a sequence of numbers, such as "123456"? Do you automatically click all links and download all email attachments coming from your friends? This book will show you just how incredibly lucky you are that nobody's hacked you before, including:

- How the internet is held together with a pinky swear

- How hackers use raunchy photos to eke out private information

- Examples of preposterous social engineering attacks

- Equally preposterous defense from those attacks

- How people in charge don't even realize what hacking means

- How there's only one surefire way to protect against hacking

- Research on past, present, and future hacking methods

- Difference between good and bad hackers

- How to lower your exposure to hacking

- Why companies pester you to attach a phone number to an account

- Why social media is the most insecure way to spend your afternoon

With this handy little book as your starting point, you can finally go from a starry-eyed internet user to a paranoid cybersecurity geek. With plenty of examples, this book will show you that the internet is not merely a way to watch cute cat videos; it's a battlefield, a military invention that was accidentally found to be capable of overpowering any threat economically, digitally and politically. From the crudest forums to the most sophisticated online services, there is a war going on and, whether you want it or not, you're involved by the very fact you're here, so better arm yourself with knowledge.

Chapter 1 – Basics of Cybersecurity

What's the best way to secure a house against burglary? A typical burglar would scope out the premises beforehand to find the easiest point of access: a garage door that won't shut all the way or a second story open window, but a brash one might just walk to the front door and work the doorknob. The house owner who's been burglarized would then want to fix the garage door, put up iron bars on windows and install a brand new reinforced steel front door. All of this costs money, creates an inconvenience and, most importantly, attracts the attention of other potential burglars in the area – what is he or she protecting?

Securing the house thus becomes an endless game of cat and mouse, with time, money and effort invested on both sides to keep or gain *access* to restricted areas. The owner might ultimately conclude the best house security system is cheap, convenient and inconspicuous but there's no stopping a burglar who's well-funded, dedicated and left alone to tinker with a security system, so all security becomes just a deterrent. It turns out that securing a computer or a network follows the same principles as securing a house, but gaining access is easier than ever and the stakes are higher; we'll notice a missing microwave but a **hacker**, a remote cyberattacker with malicious intent, can steal all our data and keep stealing it for years without us even noticing.

This book will lay out all the essential cybersecurity principles, such as **social engineering,** a way for sly hackers to gain the trust of critical personnel and access confidential data. We're already knee-deep in electronic devices that see, hear and track everything we do but with inventions such as the **Internet of Things**, a way to imbue everyday items with an internet connection, and **machine learning**, a way for computers to update themselves, we'll see more and more daring attempts at seizing what we know and who we are, the very essence of our existence for political and economic gain.

Chapter 2 – Remote Attacker

A burglar trying to break into a house and snatch a microwave is exposed to a fairly high risk: he can leave DNA or fingerprints behind, someone could see him, or he could try to pawn the microwave to an undercover cop. However, hacking is done remotely. Thus, the attacker is free to hack away with impunity; a hacker located in another country might as well be on the other side of the moon as far as arresting him is concerned. Worse yet, a sophisticated hacker can intentionally leave behind a false trail of incriminating evidence pointing to a completely innocent party.

All the previously existing tools and methods for deterring criminals absolutely don't work against hackers, who are used to finding loopholes in existing systems. Matters aren't helped by the fact that people in charge of legislation meant to protect citizens and companies don't seem to know or care what hacking is or even how the internet works. In 2006, Republican senator Ted Stevens commented on companies seizing control over the internet and used the now-infamous phrase "internet is not a big truck; it's a series of tubes."[1] In a later chapter, we'll see that the internet is in fact *not* a series of tubes.

During the 1980s, US legislation delivered CFAA (Computer Fraud and Abuse Act), which was meant to stop hackers. Until 2011, CFAA was broadened four times, each time because – surprise, surprise – hackers found a brand-new way to gain access that wasn't covered in the previous version. In the end, CFAA got so absurd[2] that it made breaching the terms of service, those few pages we all click "agree" on without reading them, of any website hacking and thus a felony. For example, a woman lying about her weight on her dating profile was now legally a "hacker", as was a man lying about his relationship status, with the punishment up to one year in prison and up to a $100,000 fine. People trying to bypass **CAPTCHA**, the automated test used to distinguish between robots and humans, to buy tickets in bulk and resell them were also caught in the sweeping CFAA language[3]. As it turns out, figuring out who is a machine online is a long-standing problem.

Alan Turing was a mathematician and programmer in the early 20th century. He devised what's known as **Turing test** during the 1950s when work on artificial intelligence just began in earnest. The core of the Turing test is two humans and a machine in three separate rooms chatting with each other using paper slips. If a human can't distinguish between a machine and a human, the machine is then said to pass the Turing test. There is to this date no known counter to the Turing test, meaning there's no way to prove a person we're chatting with online is human. CAPTCHA does try but mostly by testing vision rather than intelligence.

CAPTCHA involves looking at an image with warped numbers and letters stricken through with squiggly lines and typing in those letters

---

[1] https://www.youtube.com/watch?v=f99PcP0aFNE

[2] https://www.wired.com/2011/11/anti-hacking-law-too-broad/

[3] https://www.wired.com/2010/11/wiseguys-plead-guilty/

and numbers in the box below the image. This was a simple and fairly useful test for stopping primitive computer programs, but hackers got so crafty at defeating it that CAPTCHA gradually had to become more and more obnoxious. In the end, it's ironic that hackers were able to solve CAPTCHA more often than humans, leading to the creation of reCAPTCHA, that involves looking at tiny squares and marking those that contain a fire hydrant, a bus, a crosswalk, etc. For now, reCAPTCHA is working, but it's only a matter of time before hackers get around it as well thanks to machine learning.

In any case, both CAPTCHA and reCAPTCHA stem from the idea that it's possible to distinguish between humans and computers online in a cheap, user-friendly and quick way. This raises two uncomfortable questions: what is it that makes us human and can computers imitate that quality? The obvious answer to those questions is – we don't know. We've now entered the deep end of the philosophical pool, and all we wanted was to post something on a forum or look at pretty pictures to have a chuckle. Let's get back to what ticket scalpers did and how they defeated CAPTCHA.

Four guys got together and formed Wiseguy Tickets, which is not a suspicious name at all, operating from Los Angeles and San Francisco to buy tickets online in bulk and resell them to ticket brokers in New Jersey at a higher price. Online ticket sellers usually put in restrictions to stop someone from hogging all the tickets, but these wiseguys adapted to all security measures to buy a total of 1 million tickets between 2002 and 2009, selling them for about $25 million in profit.

How online ticket sale usually works is that customers arriving at the website are put in a queue, and a ticket is reserved for them for a couple of minutes, during which they can figure out if they want to buy it. If not, that customer is moved to the end of the queue and priority is given to the next customer. Because some events can have all tickets sold out in a matter of minutes, it's crucial that everyone *thinks* they have a fair shot at buying one, so CAPTCHA challenges are issued to slow down those who would want to hack the system.

Wiseguys would employ powerful computers that could connect to the ticket seller thousands of times at once and issue that many requests for tickets, each time using a different **IP address**, a series of numbers that show the origin of the user. Programmers were hired to figure out how to defeat CAPTCHA, in this case by asking for the version for visually impaired users that's not as robust as the visual version. Wiseguys also used **scripts**, custom software meant to do one thing only, to fill out all the forms asking for credit card and personal information in milliseconds. By using a script that pretended to be a fumbling user trying to connect to Facebook, which also uses CAPTCHA challenges, wiseguys managed to download hundreds of thousands of challenges and employ people to solve them one by one in advance.

As each CAPTCHA challenge was loaded onto the wiseguys' computers, the file signature was recorded along with the correct solution; eventually, wiseguys could instantly solve any CAPTCHA served by the ticket vendor. This turned out to be a problem because the script was too good at solving CAPTCHA and that might raise alarms, so wiseguys tweaked it to make a mistake once in a while and appear more like a human.

The sheer scale of their operation is what helped them defeat ticket vendor's security systems, as shown by the indictment[4]. Wiseguys had employees across the US but in Eastern Europe as well, paying them $1,000-1,500 per month for their programming and administrative roles. Using about a thousand legitimate credit card numbers, wiseguys would buy whole blocks of tickets, resell them at a markup and then cancel the rest. Ticket vendors fought desperately against this kind of abuse, investing around $1 million in systems upgrade but to no avail.

---

[4] https://www.wired.com/images_blogs/threatlevel/2010/03/wiseguys-indictment-filed.pdf

Chapter 3 – Social Engineering

Let's imagine Tammy, an account manager at a bank. She loves helping clients refinance their mortgages, open accounts and settle debts but it's just that she can at times feel overwhelmed with work. One day, Tammy is absolutely overrun with clients when she gets a phone call. It's one of the bank's esteemed clients, Mark, who asks for information on one of his transactions.

"I'm currently on vacation in Aruba – I mentioned it the last time we spoke – and want to know if a transaction I made today went through."

Tammy does recall Mark mentioning it, so she glances at the call scanner and sees the number does indeed match the one in Mark's account, and his account did make a transaction today.

Apparently, it all checks out, so she says, "Yes, it went through at 9:31 a.m."

Mark politely thanks her for the information and lets Tammy get back to work.

It will be sometime later that the bank director calls up Tammy and asks her about unauthorized transactions on Mark's account. Apparently, someone attempted to clean out his account, but real Mark spotted the transactions and reversed them. The bank won't be mentioning this to anyone to avoid negative publicity, and Mark was gracious enough to agree to silence, but the director just wants to know if she had anything to do with it. Tammy then remembers the phone conversation and retells how it went – the person on the other side was polite, had the same phone number, knew information only Mark should know and could even reference details of a private conversation! How could this *not* be Mark? And how in the world could merely revealing the *time* of a transaction compromise an account?

What Tammy experienced was a classic case of social engineering in which a hacker used tidbits of information to gain her trust and have her reveal additional private information. In this way, a patient hacker could keep worming his way into a bank account until he finally gets full access and does as he pleases with the funds. Since the hacker didn't have to invest much of his time, money or effort, and wasn't actually exposing himself to being caught, this kind of solicitation for information can be done over and over again, contacting everyone until that one hapless employee spills the beans. But, hold on, how did the hacker know that Mark was going to Aruba *and* that he mentioned it to Tammy, of all people? To answer that, let's rewind a bit and take a look at how a typical social engineering attack might work from the hacker's point of view.

Let's imagine George, an outgoing fellow with a pleasant personality and a propensity for pranks. His friends would certainly be shocked if they knew *he* was the hacker that called Tammy that morning and was in fact regularly doing such hustles for a nice revenue stream. If George were pressed about what he does, he'd probably admit to it being as easy as taking candy from a baby. Contrary to what stock photos in news articles show, George doesn't wear a hoodie when he's hustling nor does he use a laptop; George has an elaborate computer rig with multiple monitors set up so he can track all of his targets in real time and essentially pranks people but takes their money doing so.

George starts off his day by making a Facebook account and filling in all the fields, so the profile seems believable. For this one, he'll use raunchy photos stolen from a Russian swimsuit model's Instagram account to get likes, followers and friends, expanding his purview of potential targets. Men will flock like crazy to his profile to pepper each image and post with positive feedback, making the profile seem lifelike and setting Facebook's "Recommend a Friend" algorithm alight.

Even if someone notices that this profile seems to be impersonating someone else and reports it to Facebook, it's in the social network's interest to let these kinds of accounts be; Facebook has been bleeding users to the point of desperation for any kind of activity, especially one that engages so many users at once and keeps them coming back for more. Besides, Facebook has over 2 billion accounts, and there are not nearly enough people hired to check user reports as it cuts into company profits. The August 2018 podcast "Post No Evil"[5] describes how Facebook employees work in sweatshop conditions, with mere three-four seconds to analyze a report before deciding on it. Even if they take down the profile, George can just make another one in a matter of minutes to keep the hustle going. If the profile stays up is when the real fun begins.

By **catfishing**, pretending to be a sexy girl eager for some companionship, George can approach one of several men that engaged with his profile and provide some affection:

"You're a real man that understands women, not like these other horndogs."

For most forlorn men, this is the kind of sentence they only hear in their dreams, and seeing the apparently real woman in the profile,

---

[5] https://www.wnycstudios.org/story/post-no-evil

they build up a perfect image of their dream woman and develop an emotional connection to it, basically falling in love with the scam. Once George has the poor fellow hooked to the positive emotions, he can have him open his heart and soul, revealing any information, including details of private conversations.

George can then threaten to reveal the conversation to the target's significant other or simply have it posted online to remain on the internet forever; for gay men, George can set up a similar profile but with male underwear model's photos. Especially if the target is a public figure with a business background, any such revelation can be devastating to the company image, tanking the stock and losing shareholders millions. What's a small sum of a couple of thousand dollars compared to that kind of loss? So, the money changes hands and the indiscretion is forgiven, but George soon learned to keep the hustle going by asking for small sums of money in exchange for nude photos and eventually learned to keep the friendship going to become an emotional outlet for these men. It's when he heard Mark talking about his bank account, Tammy and vacation in Aruba that he decided to bring his hustle to the next level.

George had used **spoofing**, concealing one's own originating information, before and found it laughably easy to make it seem that his number matched Mark's when he called Tammy; there are even websites such as SpoofTel.com[6] that let anyone spoof their caller ID for as low as 10 cents a minute, with the added option of changing the caller's voice. It did take George a dozen or so calls to different bank employees after he spoke with Tammy to finally get access to Mark's account but it doesn't matter because of how effortless it all was – George only had to be polite and seem to know what he was saying, and people basically did the hustle for him. The risk is almost nonexistent as the bank won't risk ruining their public image to catch such a piddling criminal, and Mark would certainly not want

---

[6] https://www.spooftel.com/freecall/

to be reminded or have to recount his catfishing experience to the police; thus, George gets a chance to scam another day.

It might take some years until Interpol or FBI finally catch on to George and haul him by the collar to a nearby prison on numerous fraud charges, but in the meantime, he'll keep hacking and scamming whoever is gullible enough to fall for his schemes. Note how George didn't have to use any sophisticated software or even know how to program, let alone wear a hoodie; his targets were more than willing to help him out and do whatever needed to be done. But was there anything Tammy could have done differently to thwart the hacker, help out a client in genuine need *and* distinguish between the two? As it turns out, there was.

It's an inherent human need to be agreeable and help others in need, especially when one is found in a subservient position, such as an account manager getting a phone call from a client. Of course, Tammy wants to help out Mark so that he remains her client, but it's this kindness that's exploited by George. If Tammy were certain that she's talking to a hacker, there's again very little she can do – even calling the police won't do much because there hasn't actually been any harm done and George can always claim it was just a prank. Instead of volunteering information, what Tammy can do is a subtle **identity check**, a confirmation of caller's identity, by offering *wrong* information and seeing if the caller corrects her. In fact, Tammy can do a whole series of identity checks in this way until she's absolutely certain whom she's talking with. Meanwhile, George has to either go along with whatever narrative Tammy invents or risk getting exposed.

Now let's imagine the same conversation, but this time Tammy is aware that unsavory characters are posing as clients fishing for information. So, when George calls in and tries to get information on a transaction made today, Tammy can ask:

"Was it the 8:31 a.m. one or the 8:52 a.m. one?"

When in fact it was neither. George is now put in the hot seat. His mind is racing to try to think of the best approach – silence will definitely sound suspicious but giving a wrong answer will torpedo his plans, so he blurts out:

"The latter one," and carefully listens for any kind of reaction.

Tammy sounds unfazed by his reply but now knows she might be dealing with a hacker, so she keeps asking these subtle questions and offering all the wrong details to see how the caller reacts. Meanwhile, George is relieved and thinks his plan is going swimmingly.

Tammy can concoct a story about the account being locked, investigated by the tax authority or just keep transferring George to other bank staff who are in on the plan to waste his time. Alternatively, Tammy can put him on hold for hours on end, where George will patiently wait for someone to pick the phone back up but have to eventually give up without knowing if his plan worked or not. If the entire bank staff is trained to do these identity checks, they can keep any given hacker occupied until he gives up, which is the ideal solution: without involving the police, raising any alarms or even raising a voice, George is slowly brought to a realization that crime doesn't pay and decides instead to create a highly successful Youtube channel dedicated to pranks, making him a nuisance rather than a menace.

Now let's recap the social engineering attack George attempted to do, why it worked and what is considered a successful defense against it. George first created a fake Facebook profile as a starting point for his scheme and to increase his potential victim count. Facebook abhors association with the idea of being a breeding ground for hackers and scammers but lacks users and doesn't have nearly enough people sifting through reports to find all fake accounts. Mark was thrilled to find this sexy woman who seemed genuinely interested in his day and Tammy volunteered information because the bank needed to appear customer-friendly and outgoing.

So, by leveraging Facebook's dire need for more users, Mark's dire need for emotional support and the bank's dire need for positive customer relations, George managed to access confidential information and almost got Mark's funds.

By combining the weaknesses of different systems, George was able to craft a custom **attack vector**, a way of accessing private information, that nobody could anticipate or defend against. Each weakness doesn't seem all that bad on its own, but the very problem with cybersecurity is that the internet connects many things that were never before connected and perhaps aren't even supposed to be connected to each other or anything else. The most natural response to George's attack vector would then be to isolate systems from each other, but then what's the point of things such as a Facebook account nobody can interact with or a bank without phone support?

Even if George is outed as a hacker, there's no way actually to stop him until he commits a provable crime but there is a way to *deter* him, which turns out to be a much better defense against hackers. Since George used very little time, money and effort to execute his attack, any defense that expends more of any of those three is ultimately self-defeating, so the idea would be to provide false information in a low-key way so that George never moves forward with his social engineering attacks. In short, it's wise for everyone to lie about everything over the phone and online, but in a way that legitimate users can discern the truth and easily identify themselves - similar to what Tammy did when she asked if it was the 8:31 a.m. one or the 8:52 a.m. one, when in fact, it was neither. This notion of facetiousness seems contrary to common sense and kindhearted human nature, but is the only possible way to reduce **attack surface**, one's exposure to cyberattacks, and prevent hacking.

Chapter 4 – Origins of Hacking

What does the word "hack" sound like? A dictionary would define it as "to cut with repeated or irregular blows", like with an ax. That is a fitting verb because hackers use simple tools, a little bit of effort and let inertia do the rest, nothing like the sophisticated cyberattackers Hollywood wants them to be. In action movies featuring hackers, we see a massive wall panel showing the world map and a line coursing across it.

"He's too fast. He broke through our firewall!" yells a sweating, chubby and disheveled but lovable anti-hacker while chewing on a toothpick and furiously typing on his keyboard. He chose the wrong day to quit smoking.

"Beijing, Moscow, Munich," recounts the anti-hacker for those viewers that just woke up from a coma, "he's switching IPs faster than I can track him using our satellites!" Then he throws his hands up and says, "We lost him." Add in a big, contrived countdown, preferably with some kind of ominous threat in a US metropolis, and the movie just got a whole lot of drama out of a fairly simple setting with a couple of people in a room shouting at their monitors.

Of course, a typical person unaware of hacking would appreciate this kind of action-packed portrayal of an otherwise nerdy affair as it keeps the adrenaline flowing, but there's very little truth in it – first of all, proper hacking goes by *unnoticed*. When a system gets hacked, there's no dramatic discussion, no black general shouting at the chubby anti-hacker to "speak in plain English" or even a hasty reaction because *nobody even notices*. The hack itself was more like a blip, a seemingly random glitch that resolved itself without affecting the rest of the system, and if anyone did notice it, they just shrugged and went on their merry way.

There is a good reason why Hollywood would want to present hacking as this elaborate and expensive endeavor only villains with a heavy accent engage in – no movie producer would want to teach viewers how to hack, let alone show them how easy it is. Some shows go to such an extreme that it borders on absurd, as is the case with *NCIS*[7], where two young adult characters realize they're being hacked, so they pair up on the same keyboard, randomly press keys and speak **technobabble**, supposedly technical jargon, until their supervisor, a dashing older gentleman, comes in and – unplugs the monitor.

It's hard to know how much of that scene was played for laughs but there's some truth in the fact that older people in charge of sensitive systems don't understand cybersecurity, don't care about hackers and just want to deal with palpable things. In any case, real hacking would most likely be discovered months or years after the incident and cause a lot of shame rather than drama. This is because, for all the budget spent on cybersecurity, it would turn out the hacker had used nothing more advanced than a whistle, and a toy one at that.

Phone phreaking

It was during the 1960s that the US adopted phone switchboards operated by computers: they worked faster, cheaper and, without

---

[7] https://www.youtube.com/watch?v=msX4oAXpvUE

taking a break, connected callers 24/7. It was obviously an upgrade but came with a serious flaw. As John Draper, a US Air Force electronics technician, found out, these switchboards could also be hacked into by using a toy whistle that came as a prize in a box of Cap'n Crunch cereal. The whistle itself was a cheap, plastic doohickey that sounded like the one used by sailors to signal mealtime but it could match the sounds phone switchboards were making when patching callers through[8].

Because each dialed number corresponded to a certain tone, these **phone phreaks**, hackers who attacked landline networks, could whistle a specific tune to connect to any number in the world *for free* across any number of switchboards. That's it, just walk into any phone booth or use any landline phone, whistle into the microphone and get patched through to anyone, anywhere, using any number of switchboards. The call was invisible, and there was nothing the phone company could do to stop them without shutting down the entire system that took decades and billions of dollars to deploy. In 1974, two phone phreaks took control of the entire Santa Barbara landline network and informed inbound callers that the place had been hit by a nuke[9]; they gave up when they got bored.

This was, in essence, the very first **DoS**, a denial-of-service attack that aims to disrupt the target system, but the call was still billed to the caller, so how did these phone phreaks avoid astronomical charges? They would first dial a toll-free phone number and then use the whistling method to hijack the line and dial whatever the number they wanted. One long, flat whistling sound at a certain frequency reset the phone line and essentially gave the caller **admin privilege**, meaning total control of the phone call. The phone company had automated the system to ignore any calls connecting to toll-free phone numbers, so phone phreaks could do as they pleased.

---

[8] https://youtu.be/FlHN-9S9VWo?t=1077

[9] https://www.lifehacker.com.au/2015/11/the-hacker-who-inspired-apple-john-captain-crunch-draper/

John Draper started mass-producing blue boxes, small contraptions that generated tones but had a keypad or a rotary dial and could bypass the normal toll collection by the telephone company. Two entrepreneurs, both named Steve, would also start producing blue boxes and later formed a company named Apple, hiring John to help them out with their Apple computer that initially had the option of making phone calls. Thankfully, they realized the legal heat of messing with a telecom monopoly, so they switched over to productive uses for a computer. Mafia soon embraced the blue box technology to make invisible calls and even **yippies**, radical hippies, wanted to deny The Man his cut of taxes on long-distance calls.

In 1971, the Esquire magazine published an article "Secrets of the Little Blue Box"[10], which portrayed the blue box technology in such a fantastic way that anyone reading the article simply had to try it out. That's when phone phreaking entered the public consciousness, and the law enforcement agencies finally had to dial in to put an end to everyone exploiting the phone network, including the hobbyist phone phreaks. Up to that point, the law enforcement didn't want to become the collection agency of a private phone company, but now it was a matter of great urgency.

What's interesting is how phone phreaking suddenly became a crime, and those same hobbyists were suddenly treated just like mobsters. John Draper would serve multiple jail sentences for his phone phreaking, later becoming a security advisor who was the first to come up with the idea of hiring hackers to test a system against intrusion – they'll hack anyway so why not help them earn a living and help out a company by doing so?

As one phone phreak told the writer of the Esquire article, "The bigger the phone company gets and the further away from human operators it gets, the more vulnerable it becomes to all sorts of phone phreaking." This is an apt description of the concept of attack

---

[10] http://www.lospadres.info/thorg/lbb.html

surface, exposure to hacking that increases as the system becomes more complex, but also shows just how bungling big companies are when dealing with electronic systems.

John Draper realized the power in blue boxes, theorizing that three or four people armed with advanced models that outpaced the phone company hardware could block out all phone lines between any two major cities with ease. He became so paranoid that he traveled the nation, hooking up his blue box at desert highway phone booths where nobody could see him to make free calls for days, dialing random numbers across the world before disappearing like the wind.

For John and the majority of original phone phreaks the motivation wasn't to mess with the system or disrupt the lives of citizens but simply to see how the computers and machinery connecting the calls worked. Dry science beneath the phone system became vividly real, and these reclusive students of numbers and digital doodads suddenly wielded enormous power, apparently including the ability to launch nuclear missiles, again using just a whistle. To learn more about that let's get introduced to Kevin Mitnick, probably the world's most notorious hacker.

Kevin grew up in Los Angeles during the 1960s and was raised by a single mom waitress who often left him to his devices. Riding a bus every day, he soon realized a security flaw in the way bus drivers marked bus tickets – passengers who changed destination mid-route had their tickets punched in a particular way using a special punch tool. By making friends with a bus driver, Kevin soon found out where to get that tool and memorized all the punch patterns for all the routes. Visiting the trash bin at the bus terminal yielded half-used books of blank bus tickets, giving Kevin the ability to ride the bus throughout the entire San Fernando Valley for free as much as he wanted. It was in high school that Kevin first made friends with a kid who was a phone phreak.

After absorbing all the details of how phone switchboards worked, Kevin soon knew more about the phone company operation than any of its employees. As Kevin developed his hacking skills, the course of his life was set and quickly he'd get involved with other hackers, who were breaking into computer and phone systems of companies just to see if it can be done. At one point Kevin would get challenged by his fellow hackers to hack into a software company and gain access to the operating system they were developing.

By dialing the system administrator, Kevin presented himself as one of the lead managers on the project and claimed he couldn't log into his account. The administrator reset his account and helped him log in. Just like that, Kevin used social engineering to access this highly restricted and sensitive system that should have been protected at all costs. When he showed that to his hacker friends, they reacted with shock and asked for proof. It would be Kevin's turn to be shocked when his hacker friends used the account he procured to steal the operating system code and then reported Kevin to the software company as being the one responsible for the hack.

From one life story to the next, Kevin will show an amazing acuity in spotting security flaws and using social engineering attacks to discover secrets but never actually causing harm or breaking the law. Kevin would later settle down and start his own business that tested security systems of companies, often using social engineering attacks. In Chapter Three of his 2012 book, *The path of least resistance*[11], Kevin explains how he used social engineering to hack his way into Motorola's software department in 1992 and obtain the source code of their brand-new MicroTac Ultra Lite cell phone for the sake of it. To those who paid attention during our Tammy and George conversation, this will sound strikingly similar.

Kevin starts off by finding the phone number of the project manager, Sam. By calling her, Kevin gets to her voicemail and finds out Sam is on vacation, but her assistant, Alice, can handle any work-related requests. Kevin then calls Alice, presents himself as "Rick", a

---

[11]
https://cdn2.hubspot.net/hubfs/241394/SagarinMitnick2012.pdf?t=1539787791720

Motorola researcher, and asks for the latest version of the source code. Alice is more than willing to help, but it turns out she has no clue how to send out files or even compress them into an archive, so she goes to ask her security supervisor.

Kevin spends a few agonizing moments waiting for her reply but is relieved when the supervisor turns out to be eager to provide help and actually gives them his own account credentials to log into and send the file over. After a little while, Kevin now has several versions of the source code but reaches even deeper and kindly asks Alice to send a couple of files that contain passwords, IP addresses and other info related to that department. With that in hand, Kevin thanks Alice and hangs up. Now for the hacking into the facility proper.

Kevin checks the local weather reports for the facility location and waits until there's a severe snowstorm. This will provide him with ample excuse why he needs remote access. In the meantime, he extracts names, usernames and encrypted passwords from the files Alice sent over. Names and usernames are stored in **plaintext**, the kind of text humans can read, but passwords are encrypted using a one-way process that basically scrambles them. The real problem is in the **authenticator**, a small pager-like device each Motorola employee is given called SecureID. Logging into the Motorola system requires a fixed username and a SecureID code that changes every 60 seconds. Kevin either has to acquire an authenticator, which would cause an alarm, or convince someone in the facility to let him use theirs. The latter option is easier, so that's what he goes with.

After choosing a plausible name from the file Alice sent over, Kevin calls the Motorola facility posing as "Ed Bell" and asks a programmer, Ron, for help with logging into his account.

"This darn snowstorm," says Kevin. "Anyway, I left my SecureID in my office desk, top left drawer. Would you be so kind as to go fetch it and read the code for me?" Kevin counts on Ron being a typical programmer, shy and unwilling just to go and rummage through someone's office drawer but it's still a gamble – Kevin has no idea if Ed Bell actually has a top-left desk drawer or if there's anything in it.

Everything could fall apart right here, but Kevin is playing a smart game because he intentionally made an unreasonable request that he knows is unlikely to be met. When Ron hesitates, Kevin issues a smaller request that is now more likely to be met – why not help a fellow programmer out and let him use your account to log in? In what is a typical sales tactic, Kevin pushes until getting his foot in the door, so to speak, and then seemingly backs down to a smaller request that is still unreasonable, but the victim feels compelled to give in and help out.

Ron agrees to share his account with Kevin but warns that he'll have to ask his security supervisor about it. Kevin waits with bated breath while Ron dials the supervisor and finally lets a sigh of relief as Ron vouches for him, "Yeah, I know Ed."

In-group preference, the notion of valuing people who belong to our own group more than outsiders, is a powerful motivator that gives an air of authority to Kevin and lets him push for even more access and sensitive data.

Ron finally hangs up and says, "The supervisor wants to have a word with you."

Kevin will now do the same trick he just did with Ron, but with the added help of in-group preference, asking the supervisor, "Can't you just let Ron fetch my SecureID? It's in the top left drawer." As expected, the supervisor refuses, so Kevin issues a smaller request, "Can I then use someone else's account to log in? It's just over the weekend, and my deadline is brutal."

Supervisor mulls over it for a moment and finally agrees, even letting Ron help out Kevin with whatever else he needs doing.

Finally getting access to the Motorola server, Kevin can look into different systems to find the best target. He still doesn't have access to the cell phone system, so he scans IP addresses on the server and finds a workstation that will let him try out different passwords. He hits the password file Alice gave him with a **dictionary attack**, a simple program that tries to guess passwords by going through a list of simple words and most common passwords. The file shows three users who use that workstation, one of whom is John Cooper. Dictionary attack finally strikes gold and shows a match: John apparently had used "mary" as his password at some point, but it's no longer working.

Kevin goes into the phone book and finds John Cooper's number. By pretending to be a recovery technician who just had a server failure at the Motorola facility, Kevin can use all the details and names he discovered so far to concoct a plausible story that explains why all the urgency and also override John's normal sense of judgment. By offering to help with setting up a new account for John, Kevin subtly mentions the old password from the file he got from Alice and John finally believes him, revealing his new password, "bebop1", that finally lets Kevin log into the Motorola system.

In any case, Kevin Mitnick aimed at never causing direct damage to systems and companies he hacked, instead focusing on simply investigating how they work, just like John Draper did. In 1994, *The New York Times* ran a front-page story on Kevin Mitnick, calling him "computer programmer run amok". This turned Kevin Mitnick from a young hacker prodigy into public enemy number one, later earning the writer of that article, John Markoff, more than a million dollars thanks to a book deal on Kevin and the hacker culture. According to Kevin, it was his refusal to participate in a 1991 ready-made movie deal that angered John and launched a vendetta. Thus, began the smear campaign on Kevin that will indelibly stain the rest of his life.

Chapter 5 – Principles of Social Engineering

The two social engineering attacks that Kevin Mitnick performed to break into the Motorola facility used **six principles of persuasion** by Dr. Robert Cialdini, a professor of psychology from Arizona State University. His 1984 book, *Influence: The Psychology of Persuasion*, described the six most common ways to gain trust or rather act on people to make them do what we want.

The first principle is *reciprocity*, the idea that doing a favor for someone earns us their gratitude and they ought to repay in kind, even if they didn't ask for the initial favor. This is most likely a survival instinct, where we fear being abandoned by others, especially those who are kindhearted, and want to keep them by our side. Companies use this principle by giving out free samples or other token goodies that make customers feel obliged to buy their product.

The second principle is *commitment and consistency*. Everyone likes a good story, so when we find a good story that sounds consistent, we get committed to making it sound right. This explains why people would help out Kevin – as soon as he got them to commit to a story, they would go out of their way to make it consistent and overlook any strange details. By subtly pushing people to commit to a story, Kevin already got them hook, line and sinker.

The third principle is *social proof*. If we're introduced to someone in some capacity, they're more likely to believe it than if we were to present ourselves as such. When Kevin got the trust of Alice and Ron, they vouched for him to their security supervisors, who were more willing to accept Kevin's odd request for SecureID. This is what we can call "peer pressure", the idea that we'll want to blend into the group and do whatever people around us are doing. In advertisements, this is used whenever there is a group of people shown, and one of them is accepted into the group because of clothes, snacks, toys, etc.; the message is that buying a product gives social proof.

The fourth principle is *authority*. Being a leader means making tough choices that draw attention, so by simply following the leader, people avoid responsibility in making the choices themselves or being criticized. By asserting himself as a team member and correctly timing a few key phrases, Kevin got accepted as one by the security supervisors, who were probably relieved that Kevin seemed to know what he was doing and didn't have to be babysat.

The fifth principle is *liking*. When we have an established relationship with someone, they are more likely to give in to further requests. This is why advertisements use pretty and likable people to promote products – we're more likely to buy a product if we feel attracted to the person promoting it.

The sixth principle is *scarcity*. People are more likely to ignore caution if they're led to believe they have a limited time to act or if buying a product makes them a member of some sort of privileged circle. Advertisements exploit this desire to be ahead of everyone else by promising limited-time discounts.

All six of these principles are used continuously on the general public by companies pushing their services or products, but we've now seen hackers use them as well. These six principles could be considered ways to hack the human brain. Luckily, Dr. Cialdini presents ways to defend oneself from all six of these principles and realize when we're being pushed into doing something we don't actually want to do. Paraphrased, the defense goes like this:

When dealing with someone pushing for favors, we should ask ourselves, "Has anyone asked me to do this kind of favor before?" If yes, then what was the outcome of doing that favor? Did we feel good about helping? If no one has asked for this kind of favor before, is the person asking for it acting in good faith, and are they genuinely in need of help or do they have an agenda? According to Dr. Cialdini, resisting psychological pressure done through these six principles boils down to checking our gut instinct and going along with it, no matter how much authority we're facing.

Humans are social creatures, with social norms etched into our brains since early childhood. We're eager to help; we want to share and can't allow a fellow human suffer due to our inaction. The problem arises when those same mannered people have to handle sensitive information and can't distinguish between what's private and what's public. All social engineering attacks rely on evoking emotions to the point the victim forgets about security and lets the cat out of the bag, so to speak.

Chapter 6 – Ethical Hacking

Kevin Mitnick would eventually get arrested with the help of blank warrants, put into solitary confinement without a bail hearing and have to waive his Constitutional rights. The die was cast, and the government was now committed to prosecuting and persecuting Kevin at all costs. Media could simply quote the defamatory statements from *The New York Times'* story, and Kevin had no way to refute any of it, except when he went to trial after eight months in solitary confinement. The prosecutor will claim Kevin caused $300 million in damages by breaking into software companies, though none of them ever reported any losses, as it's required by law. Details of Kevin's alleged crimes are still sealed, supposedly to cover up gross negligence by the prosecutor who realized Kevin's innocent but had to follow through with the charges to save face.

Phone phreaking was still fresh in the minds of the public, so Kevin was said to be able to launch nuclear missiles by whistling into a phone, though the NORAD network is sealed off from all public phone or internet networks. Kevin was sentenced to five years in prison, couldn't profit off of any books or movies made of his experiences or even use the internet, cell phones or radio for several years. John Markoff would later write a book, *Takedown*, about Kevin Mitnick that eventually become a movie of the same name, starring Tom Berenger. If Kevin did nothing wrong, why was he punished so harshly?

The thing is that laws usually consider intention and the context of what happened. For example, smacking someone in the face with a basketball can be a mishap or an assault depending on if it happened on the court or in the street but laws concerning hacking ignore intention and context completely. One possible explanation is that legislators are vaguely aware of hacking but consider it a nuisance – until there's a highly visible hacker that can be made an example of. There's obviously a difference between wiseguys who hogged all the tickets to make money and Kevin who just wanted to take a peek, but legally, the two are equally reprehensible.

So we come to the ethics of hacking and two broad categories: white hat and black hat hacking. The names come from Western movies, where a viewer could easily spot the villain and the hero based off of their hats. **White hat hacking** has the intention of scouting a computer system and seeing it from the inside out of sheer curiosity but can also include hackers hired by the company to test its systems and users annoyed by petty limitations of software they're using. **Black hat hacking** is malicious, done with the intent to cause damage. For example, to steal credit card information or to make a competitor site unresponsive. The hat metaphor goes deeper because it shows that *the same hacker can switch roles as easily as switching hats*.

In some cases, the lines blur and users are forced to resort to a mix between white and black hat hacking just to make software usable. One notable example of this was Mozilla Firefox browser, which provided a robust framework for users to program small pieces of code called **plugins** that added extra functionality to the browser. There were literally thousands of plugins, called "add-ons" by Mozilla, for all sorts of purposes, giving each user the chance to customize their version of Firefox. It all went splendidly until some black hat hackers decided to bury **trojans**, malware that gives covert access to the infected machine, inside these plugins[12] and Mozilla decided to clamp down on how they can be used.

Hands down the best plugin for Firefox was Adblock Plus, a terrific add-on that blocked all ads and also allowed the user to write his or her own filters for blocking whatever else was bothersome: images, code, frames, etc. Adblock Plus gave Firefox users a tremendous amount of power in deciding what they wanted to see and the decision was unanimous – ads are awful. The problem is, ad revenue is the lifeblood of many websites and companies, including Google. An Adblock user that comes to a website is essentially using it for free, so companies started including anti-Adblock scripts in their websites, to which the users responded by creating anti-anti-Adblock scripts[13].

Ad companies eventually went for the jugular and approached the maker of Adblock Plus with a simple offer – here's a blank check, and you tell us what to do to slip past the filters. The owner of Adblock Plus thus came up with the idea of "acceptable ads", simple, non-intrusive ads that don't spy on the viewer[14]. Hold on, ads spy on the viewer? Oh, they sure do. Not only that, but ads can serve malware and infect a machine while being obnoxious, all without the user even noticing.

---

[12] https://www.zdnet.com/article/mozilla-firefox-hit-by-malware-add-ons/

[13] https://www.techspot.com/news/63799-anti-adblock-killer-extension-prevents-sites-blocking-adblocks.html

[14] https://adblockplus.org/acceptable-ads#privacy-friendly-acceptable-ads

Chapter 7 – Tracking Through Cookies

What does your typical day spent online look like? You might visit a couple of Youtube channels you always watch, check out local news websites you always follow and get some entertainment from the same sources as always. The thing is, we all have our behavior patterns that change very little, offline and online: same food, same entertainment and so on. We change the rut when we experience major events, such as getting a pet, and that's what the ads are aiming for, to jump in right as we're about to have a major course correction and offer their product or service. The purpose of ads isn't to convince us to buy a product once, but to make us lifelong customers.

To do that, ad networks created a scheme to track users online and analyze their behavior, such as tracking where users click and how long they stay on each page, but first things first, let's explain cookies. Visiting a website sets a **cookie**, a small, unique text file that has legitimate uses, such as showing which links we've opened or keeping us logged in when we come back to the site. When the internet first became popular in the 1990s, the problem websites faced was that they had no way to distinguish between users. Cookie was a solution that created a persistent identity for users; cookies worked back then, so the concept just remained and nobody really thought about what will happen when cookies get exploited.

A cookie is self-contained and can only be read by the website that created it. Cookies typically last for ten years and are removed only when they expire on their own or when the user clears them. All private information in a cookie, the user entered, such as form data or username and password combination that logs him or her into a website; everything else is called **metadata**, or data on data. The way ad networks hacked cookies is by realizing that *a cookie is set if merely a single pixel is requested from a website*. This means that an ad company can embed slivers of its content all across the internet and create a comprehensive surveillance grid that knows every move of every visitor.

To keep things simple, let's say Coca-Cola hires an ad company to serve soda ads online. The ad company approaches websites, such as CNN.com, and pays a couple of cents for each unique view and a bit more for each ad click that leads to a purchase of soda. CNN gets millions of visits, so now only has to write engaging and truthful content to keep people coming. Thus, users get interesting content, Coca-Cola gets to sell soda, but ad companies have the biggest task – they have to psychologically profile users to figure out which ad is the most appropriate and justify the millions that Coca-Cola gave them. So far, it's all pretty innocuous, but we're about to see how quickly this gets out of hand.

Now let's imagine John, a typical internet user. John visits CNN.com and gets served CNN's and 20 third-party cookies that have nothing to do with CNN itself but belong to websites owned by the ad company. Why? Because ads aren't on CNN itself; they are served from the ad company websites, and each sets its own cookie that doesn't have to contain any more information other than the time created, and now we've got John Smith's online presence pinpointed in time down to a millisecond.

John sees the soda ads on CNN but doesn't really feel thirsty. Now he's finished reading the article, and he goes to Youtube, which sets its own and another 20 third-party cookies, this time by different ad websites. Youtube also serves ads but let's say it partnered with Nike to sell sneakers. The ad company that partnered with Nike serves different ads and watches John's behavior – was the ad watched to the end? Did John skip it? And so on. All of this helps compile data not just on John but on his entire demographic, so if John is 32 years old, not married and loves hiking, his behavior can be used to figure out what other men of that age, marital status and hobby preference like or dislike and what kind of ad will make them open their wallet.

Repeat this process enough, and over the course of the day John received hundreds of third-party cookies, only a few of which were actually necessary to use the websites he visited; every other cookie is there to track him online by showing when he visited each website. Websites can also agree to share other data on users behind the scenes, with users completely oblivious to the fact. In this way, the two ad companies create a sprawling web of surveillance, and it all started with trying to sell soda and sneakers to make everyone happy. Now imagine this same setup increased thousandfold, with different ad companies competing for data and ad placement, and you'll get a bit closer to the real picture of what using the internet is actually like.

It's hard to overstate how much money is involved in advertising. In 2017, Pepsi made an ad[15] starring Kendall Jenner where she is shown posing a couple of times, walking and handing a can of Pepsi to another actor. She's on the screen some 30 seconds but apparently got $400,000-1,000,000 for her role. These companies have enormous budgets and can afford to drop millions on ads without

---

[15] https://people.com/food/kendall-jenner-pepsi-commercial-company-cost/

flinching, just to get a chance to penetrate another space before the competition. Imagine having a website and being approached by one of these companies with the offer of truckloads of money to place ads. It's free money and completely legal, so why not do it?

Ad companies approach millions of website owners and offer them deals through Google ad services, which let owners make money by just getting visited; thus, exposing their users' behavior. Each user over time creates a completely unique stockpile of cookies that show their every move from the moment they got the first cookie. Web browsers do allow cookies to be deleted manually and usually have a separate option to reject all cookies, but some websites will detect the latter and refuse to give access to such user. Blocking some or all cookies can also make websites unusable since it's rare that a website hosts all of its content.

So, to recap: cookies are a useful piece of technology that has become the foundation of how we use the internet, but third parties have figured out how to exploit cookies and track users. Note how we qualified these ad company cookies as being "third party", as that's the core issue in the entire cookie tracking problem. In this case, **third-party content** simply means anything served to the user without explicit permission or knowledge. For example, John visited CNN.com but got 20 third-party cookies by let's say adserve.com, adserver.com, adservices.com and so on.

By sharing content and serving a digital potpourri to users, websites have made it impossible to keep anything private or isolated; it would be like 50 ad executives listening in to every conversation you have with your friend and cutting in to offer an ad based on what you're mentioning. How is any of this cookie tracking legal? Don't websites, in this case, CNN.com, have to disclose that they're helping third parties track users? *They actually do,* it's just that nobody reads any of these privacy policies. It's quite brilliant because what would otherwise be surveillance is perfectly acceptable when the user consents.

In May 2018, EU introduced GDPR, a sweeping set of rules for websites using cookies for tracking, mandating that users have to give "informed consent", so websites simply put up a huge banner for all incoming EU users that stated, "We're tracking you using cookies." The user then dismisses it and continues being tracked. Now let's examine CNN's own privacy policy, in particular, the part where cookies are covered[16]. Privacy policies can change, but the core meaning will always stay the same. This one is current as of October 2018 and has a wall of text, but we'll just focus on the words "third party" – since that reveals the method. Ready?

"We or a *third party* platform with whom we work may place or recognize a unique cookie on your browser to enable you to receive customized content, offers, services or advertisements on our Services or other sites. These cookies contain no information *intended* to identify you personally."

You see how it's done? By simply admitting that, well, we might be tracking you but it's not *intended*, just like that, CNN is off the hook. Let's move on.

"We, our *third party* service providers, advertisers, advertising networks and platforms, agencies, or our Partners also may use cookies or other tracking technologies to manage and measure the *performance of advertisements* displayed on or delivered by or through the Turner Network and/or other networks or Services. This also helps us, our service providers and Partners provide more relevant advertising."

There's the admission that the user behavior is being analyzed to make better ads. There's just one more paragraph, and we're done.

"Syncing Cookies and Identifiers. We may work with our Partners (for instance, *third party* ad platforms) to *synchronize* unique, anonymous identifiers (such as those associated with cookies) in

---

16 https://edition.cnn.com/privacy0?no-st=9999999999#turner_cookies

order to match our Partners' uniquely coded user identifiers to our own."

Can you see it? There are user profiles made based on what was visited on CNN and other websites and compared behind the scenes with what the ad company knows about the user.

We mentioned Youtube so let's examine its cookie policy. By visiting Youtube.com and scrolling all the way down, there's this tiny link titled "Privacy" with a lot of good info, but this is a video site, so search for "A look at cookies" and hear Google's engineer Maile Ohye explain cookies almost the same way we did at the start of this chapter. Overall, Google has put a lot of effort into being honest with its users and is probably the most transparent company when it comes to tracking. One thing you'll notice is few mentions of third-party services and companies. This is because Google *is* the third party. Google has become so big in the ad business that they command the market and they also allow users to control these hidden ad profiles to an extent by visiting the My Activity section of their Google account.

Google also hosts content, such as snippets of code, to help website owners save money on bandwidth. Isn't that wonderful? Remember what we said about cookies – if a single pixel is requested from a third-party website, it gets to set its cookie, so by hosting content, Google gets a much broader peek into browsing habits of users. When Youtube videos are embedded into pages, the cookie is set too, but Facebook, LinkedIn, and other social media do something similar with their embedded Like and Share buttons, all of which can be blocked with Adblock Plus. This covers cookies, now let's examine other content found on websites, such as Javascript.

Chapter 8 – Javascript and Flash

The early 1990s were the time when the internet and everything related to computers was just starting to take off, so everyone experimented to see what they can come up with. One such invention was Javascript, a dynamic programming language. The main draw of Javascript was the ability to change the page as the user was interacting with it. You know all those banners that follow you around the page? That's Javascript. Resizing comment boxes? Javascript. Visiting your favorite website and clicking on content to enlarge it? You get the picture.

Javascript is everywhere and apparently can do everything, which is how websites gradually started including it where it doesn't belong. **Cross-site scripting**, a way for hackers to inject third-party Javascript into target websites and have it executed in any computer browser that visits it, was first noticed in the early 2000s. Now it applies to all sorts of code, but it initially referred to Javascript, so that's the context we'll use it in.

Cross-site scripting or XSS, abbreviated like that because X is much cooler than C, relies on the fact browsers typically check for three things when deciding whether to accept or refuse content: entire web address, name of the host and IP address. All content that matches the same three conditions is treated the same, so XSS finds weaknesses in trusted websites to inject its own code into whatever is being served to the browser. Browsers can fight this in several ways, one of which is **sandboxing**, or separating every browser tab in its own bubble that can't affect anything else. Sandboxing is the main reason why browsers, Google Chrome in particular, use so much RAM memory.

Even sandboxing might not be enough in the future, as the **Row Hammering** attack looks at jumping the **air gap**, the distance between two physically separate components[17]. As technology advances, hardware gets smaller and denser, containing more components in less space. Past a certain point, these components start becoming very sensitive to nearby influences, which is exploited by Row Hammering. A common RAM stick refreshes its state millions of times a second, usually denoted by its frequency in megahertz (MHz). By making these tiny components refresh much faster and with greater coordination than they're accustomed to, Row Hammering induces RAM errors that, with some luck, can be exploited to make the operating system load wrong files and thus malware.

When all you have is electronics, all attack vectors start getting named after hammers. **Powerhammer** is a way to jump the air gap and send data outside through the power cable[18] in cases where

---

[17] https://nakedsecurity.sophos.com/2015/03/12/row-hammering-how-to-exploit-a-computer-by-overworking-its-memory/

[18] https://boingboing.net/2018/04/13/bridgeware-vs-airgaps.html

malware is already on the airgapped machine. By precisely timing the workload of a machine, it can be made to draw more or less power, and the outside party can stand by a power service panel to read the fluctuations and receive data at a rate of 120 bytes a second.

An XSS attack could look like this – there is a search box on a website. When visitors type in a word, such as "car" or "door", the website does the search and returns the results. If a piece of Javascript code is searched for, the website, depending on how it's built, goes haywire and can be made to execute the third-party code. On its own, this isn't that scary, but just like we saw with George the catfisher, it's about combining security weaknesses in several related systems that make hacks devastating. If this kind of malformed link pointing to bizarre search results is shared with gullible people – for example, those being catfished on Facebook or Tinder – there is a huge chance someone will fall for it and click the link. Then the rest depends on the code, which can steal cookies, install trojans and so on.

Firefox users can run NoScript, an add-on that allows the user to block some or all Javascript from executing. One nice feature of NoScript is that it lets the user peek under the hood as the page is loading and running to see just how Javascript actually works. Another relevant add-on is called **Greasemonkey**, an add-on that lets you inject code directly into your browser as you're using it. So, you can write your own code or copy someone's and run it through Greasemonkey to immediately change how websites work and feel on your end, such as changing the background color, zooming in or out, etc.

Google has decided to use Javascript for added security starting November 2018, requiring all users logging into Google services to have Javascript enabled[19]. The idea is that hackers use stripped-down versions of browsers to run hundreds of them at once; these tools

---

[19] https://security.googleblog.com/2018/10/announcing-some-security-treats-to.html

would supposedly pick up on that and deny a login, even if done with a proper username and password.

Cookies and Javascript are typically small morsels of data and don't impact browser performance, but an avalanche of both makes the browser grind to a halt, and the dreaded "loading" spinner shows up: you can't click anything, you can't close the tab, go back or do much of anything except hold still or restart the machine. Cookies and Javascript files also fill up the hard drive, which isn't a big deal at first but it all adds up. To make matters worse, this torrent of data hogs your bandwidth, which is usually capped in the US, literally wasting the user's money to ineffectively spy on them. It's not the first time previously glorified technology became a burden, as evidenced by Adobe Flash.

Flash was originally used by Adobe as a rich framework for animation, such as online video games; even Youtube used Flash to deliver videos. The intention behind Flash was to make it the golden standard of online animation with possibilities of encrypting Flash content to disable sharing and make each customer fork out cash for a separate copy of content but that never panned out. Hackers ripped Flash apart to find numerous security flaws, each of which Adobe had to patch at its own expense. In the end, Flash was everywhere, slowed machines, annoyed users with autoplay videos and represented a security risk. All major browsers have transitioned away from Flash, and Adobe will finally be able to breathe a sigh of relief in 2020 when Flash is no longer supported.

Chapter 9 – Browser Wars

There's a reason why this book is emphasizing Firefox and its add-ons so much; it's probably the closest we've ever got to a perfect browser for hackers, a browser made *for* users *by* users. Firefox got into the limelight when Internet Explorer held the internet in an iron grip, and Google Chrome was just a twinkle in an engineer's eye. Back then, Microsoft established a solid monopoly on all Windows computers and mandated Internet Explorer be installed – browsers had to be bought back then – to the point the US government had to step in and break up the company.

Firefox is an **open-source** browser, meaning anyone can review its code, download, share it and even tweak it to make their own version, which people have done to produce forks, such as Cyberfox, Waterfox, Palemoon and so on. Each of these versions prioritizes some Firefox features over others, trying to get curb **feature creep**, the incessant desire of software developers to expand and upgrade their software. Feature creep is in large part responsible for increasing the attack surface in all software.

Mozilla, the company that made Firefox, no longer has the same priorities it once had and by all accounts is somewhat ashamed of how hacker-friendly Firefox became, so it's been clamping down on what can be done with add-ons. Since 2010, Firefox underwent several radical makeovers as Mozilla desperately tried to move into mainstream consciousness as a newbie-friendly browser, even going so far as to oust co-founder **Brendan Eich**, the very creator of Javascript, over a minor personal opinion in 2014. Firefox is still leaps and bounds ahead of what Internet Explorer, called Edge on Windows 10, Opera, Safari and Chrome allow, as they're all proprietary browsers that run on proprietary code and have corporate weight to press anyone trying to modify it or, God forbid, make money off of those modifications.

Broadly speaking, under Mozilla Public License 2.0[20] any person is free to make money off of any Firefox code as long as that same freedom is forwarded to all customers. Google Chrome's terms of service[21], however, forbid you from even looking inside its source code to know what's happening; this is the standard "forbidden to reverse engineer" clause. You can still do it in secret, but if Google finds out, you risk being permanently banned from all their platforms and denigrated as a vile hacker that wants to launch nukes.

The closed source nature of Google Chrome turned out to be a problem in 2015, when Google decided to install a microphone component that listened to the words "Ok, Google" to trigger a web search[22]. So, how was this discovered? Google Chrome has an open source twin called Chromium, and it was the addition of this Hotword module to it that revealed something fishy. Official reply

---

[20] https://www.mozilla.org/media/MPL/2.0/index.815ca599c9df.txt

[21] https://www.google.com/chrome/privacy/eula_text.html

[22] https://www.privateinternetaccess.com/blog/2015/06/google-chrome-listening-in-to-your-room-shows-the-importance-of-privacy-defense-in-depth/

by the engineer that created the module[23] was that there's a checkbox for opting into Hotword, so it's not a really big deal. Besides, if you're already using Chrome or Chromium, you're trusting Google, so why not trust it with Hotword? Safe to say that this incident didn't instill confidence in those Chrome or Chromium users who understood that this was an actual breach of security; the rest had no clue because all the updates are done silently, and they just click "OK" and "I agree" on any dialog boxes anyway.

Let's go back to our John Smith who's happily surfing the web. John is using Firefox for entertainment and Chrome for work at the same time, and they're both working as expected. John is happy, and all is well with the world. What's this? A popup appears: *Firefox wants to... Yes or no?* At the same time, Chrome blinks in the taskbar: *Chrome has updated... Yes or no?* John is flustered, his workday is ruined, and he now has to actually read, *think* and act based on his thought process. John suddenly wakes up and sits bolt upright; it was just a nightmare. That's not how browsers work today because they're all **evergreen**, constantly shifting masses of code that hide all meaningful decisions away from the user's prying eyes.

Users are still given an illusion of control, mostly over meaningless, repetitive and tiresome tasks, such as dismissing the same dialog box over and over again. This is a real security issue when coupled with **banner blindness**[24], the propensity of software users to ignore the same shape that's been proven unworthy of their attention. We all have a limited attention span and an innate system that uses peripheral vision to determine whether content is worthy of our attention, so constantly seeing the same shape that does nothing invokes a powerful reflex to dismiss it without looking. Advertisements try to hack this system by flashing, blaring, moving, changing size and so on to attract attention, but hackers too can exploit banner blindness by bundling a harmful or insecure program

---

[23] https://news.ycombinator.com/item?id=9735795

[24] https://www.youtube.com/watch?v=Ghtog0yAXE0

with something trusted and hoping the user approves or installs them together by sheer force of habit.

Piggyback programs, additional software generally not disclosed when the bundle was downloaded, rely on this reflex to get installed. **Trialware** generally promises great utility and lets you use it for a little bit only to suddenly shut down with "your trial period has expired" or "that is only available to premium users". **Adware** actually embeds ads in the program, this often being a browser toolbar, or shows them directly on the desktop. **Spyware** leeches data off of a user's machine, such as by installing a **keylogger**, a program that monitors user keyboard presses to capture banking information, usernames and passwords. Otherwise, the piggyback program can be straight up malware.

So, how did we get to evergreen software? Programming in the 1990s and prior was done on a static basis, that's to say a team of engineers working for a software company would get an idea and work on it until the product was ready to stand on its own. The internet was scarce back then so software, especially one users paid for, had to work out of the box. Users would keep using that software way past its expiration date, opening themselves to hackers and potentially directing negative publicity at the software company but also not coming back to buy the latest and greatest version. With the advent of the internet, those same engineers can remain gainfully employed working on the same piece of software until kingdom come because now – it's meant to be evergreen.

Constantly changing software thwarts attack vectors, disables plugins, keeps successful software on the market and allows engineers to miss deadlines because hey, we've got the internet and we'll put it in the next update. Thanks to the evergreen update scheme, Firefox is already on version 63, with six-seven new versions being released every year; at this rate, Firefox will reach version 100 around the year 2023 and 200 around 2037. Whenever you've had a problem with software, and someone told you to "check for updates" as a solution, the problem was in evergreen software, half-baked piles of code that occasionally worked. But there's still a major problem – that of evergreen software being used by actual people who have to consent to updates in some manner.

So, evergreen software takes away control over what, when and how code is installed and just does updates silently, which is how Chrome, Opera and Firefox all work. Operating systems and productivity suites do this too; Windows 10 is evergreen, and so is Office 365. When the entire computer holds nothing but evergreen software, conflicts are bound to happen, in which case we just – update everything again. Behold, the glorious evergreen software! By the way, that new feature isn't working. There will be an update coming soon.

Revealing what an update does exposes the source code, tasks engineers with documenting their code, which is a sore point in itself, and burdens the user with text he or she is not likely to understand. Besides, what if there's a crucial update and the user refuses to install it, perhaps because they don't need that one plugin? By adopting the notion of **security through obscurity**, the idea that software nobody understands can't be exploited, software makers lull themselves into complacency. Security through obscurity represents what's known as **mitigation defense**[25], meaning that hacking attacks are accepted as inevitable, so the focus is on just hiding as much data as possible to minimize the severity of any given hack attack. It's just simple math done in accounting: preventing hacker attacks costs millions, but mitigation defense merely destroys user trust, so that's what the company will go with.

Security through obscurity does tend to discourage **script kiddies**, usually young adults who have no clue about hacking but have somehow gotten ahold of scripts and are running them to see what happens. They are usually easy to thwart, sometimes by simply

---

[25] https://www.darkreading.com/attacks-breaches/damage-mitigation-as-the-new-defense/d/d-id/1137451

changing the default values in a program. One example[26] given by Jesper Johansson, senior Microsoft engineer in charge of security, is renaming all Administrator accounts on a network to something else, such as "Janitor". This makes all scripts that rely on hacking into "Administrator" account fail while triggering an alarm. Another solution is creating a **honeypot**[27], an intentionally open network or server with some glaring vulnerabilities and apparently valuable data; by placing a scanner in a honeypot, the attacks are monitored and logged.

It just so happens that evergreen software can't be audited by the public to see if it's worth the money, copied by the competition or analyzed by researchers to see if it has any **backdoors**, hidden access points not available to legitimate users. As we've seen so far, hackers excel at revealing secrets and connecting the dots to exploit shared weaknesses, but the ones hurting are legitimate users who don't care about hacking; they are left with opaque software that constantly updates. All this means is that when **bugs**, unintended code interactions, and backdoors do get revealed, there's a firestorm of criticism and panic before everyone settles down and keeps using the same software, now updated.

In 1999, Windows NT operating system received its fifth service pack but with some apparently unintended additions. One security researcher, Andrew Fernandez, examined a standard Windows driver used for securing files and connections, ADVAPI.DLL, and inside found labels named "key" and "NSAkey". He concluded that the National Security Agency (NSA) was responsible for surveillance of communications, was in cahoots with Microsoft and managed to slip in its own key that could be used as a backdoor to all Windows NT

---

[26] https://docs.microsoft.com/en-us/previous-versions/technet-magazine/cc510319%28v=msdn.10%29

[27] https://www.sans.edu/cyber-research/security-laboratory/article/honeypots-guide

systems[28]. Through sheer laziness, or perhaps arrogance, someone forgot to remove the labels; thus, revealing the existence of the second key.

Microsoft will meekly deny[29] any foul play with: "Microsoft does not leave 'back doors' in our products", though its own engineers who worked on Windows NT will react with shock when researchers face them with the discovery of a *third* key in the next version of the operating system, Windows 2000. The reason why they didn't know what the software they made contains is **compartmentalization**, splitting of an assignment into small parcels so that nobody has the big picture, which would explain all the bugs and problems native to Windows.

The real problem is that these kinds of backdoors can be *turned against the intelligence agencies that installed them*. It doesn't matter how well they're hidden; they're a ticking time bomb. Once they're out in the wild, ten or 15 years later some child prodigy will MacGyver toothpicks and paperclips to easily unlock the key and, since there will still be agencies and companies using these operating systems, easily hack them and keep hacking them over the course of years. This is on top of government employees already having derisible cybersecurity awareness.

---

[28] https://www.heise.de/tp/features/How-NSA-access-was-built-into-Windows-3444341.html

29

https://web.archive.org/web/20000520001558/http://www.microsoft.com/security/bulletins/backdoor.asp

Chapter 10 – State-sponsored Malware

Over the course of years, a hacker group named **Turla** managed to breach the security of several EU governments to leech confidential information. A late 2017 German cybersecurity audit revealed a compromised version of Microsoft Outlook deployed by Turla in several departments as far back as late 2016. Analysis of how the attack went[30] is a fascinating read: by using **phishing**, an attack that makes the target think they're using a trusted website, link or service, Turla deployed several stages of trojans, each providing gradually more access until they could exploit a weakness in Microsoft Outlook that allowed them to read all emails sent to and from the infected machine.

Malware is split into several types depending on what it's meant to do: **viruses** make the machine unusable, trojans provide a backdoor, **rootkit** ensures invisibility and **worms** spread throughout a network.

---

[30] https://www.welivesecurity.com/wp-content/uploads/2018/08/Eset-Turla-Outlook-Backdoor.pdf

In this case, the exploit relied on a little bit of trojan, rootkit and worm action to remain undetected as long as possible and inch through the network but also used an ingenious trick to communicate with Turla and even receive updates. Analysis of infected files shows that they were first made in 2009 and then gradually developed over the years. In essence, the exploit relies on the fact Outlook allows installation of custom plugins, so by finding a way to install an infected one that didn't show up in any of Outlook's menus, the exploit could scan all emails and send reports back to Turla.

Firewall, an internet filtering measure, was bypassed using encrypted PDF files sent as email attachments that could both contain commands and harvested data, such as email content and metadata. These PDF files could be opened with a PDF viewer but contained only a 1x1 pixel white image, displaying a single blank page. Automated email management systems legitimately present in Outlook were used to hide these command&control emails, so a user watching at his inbox intently could spot only a flicker of an email before the exploit deleted it without any record. Desktop notifications were also blocked. The exploit came with a list of preset email addresses where it could report back to Turla but also had a way to add backup email addresses in case the original ones were taken down.

By all accounts, Turla was a state-sponsored hacker group since their goal was mainly surveillance and monitoring rather than immediate financial gain. They showed a great deal of patience and skill, using custom encryption methods to buy as much time as possible when their exploit was ultimately discovered. An entire suite of Turla malware was eventually discovered. Among them were Trojans, used to deploy the Outlook exploit, such as Gazer[31], where the authors even put in some video game references in the code. Malware was used against states before, and this exploit was fairly tame compared to **Stuxnet**, the world's most famous cyber-weapon.

---

[31] https://www.welivesecurity.com/wp-content/uploads/2017/08/eset-gazer.pdf

Stuxnet

Iran has been a thorn in the side of the United States (US) for quite a long time. Having a prominent position in the Middle East, namely access to the Caspian Sea and the Persian Gulf, Iran is bordered by Afghanistan and Iraq, both of which have been invaded by the US since the turn of the century. Iran also happens to be a Russian ally and has been enriching nuclear material for decades, supposedly for peacetime purposes. Having access to nuclear weapons would give Iran a substantial bargaining chip and probably lead to the escalation of its anti-Israel rhetoric. It would be a real shame if something were to happen to Iranian uranium enrichment plants, say a highly sophisticated cyber-weapon would hit them in an untraceable way.

Stuxnet is a worm designed to infect computers running Windows and having Siemens uranium enrichment centrifuges attached to them. A monumental deal of thought and planning went into programming Stuxnet, as it was meant to simply spread to up to three other machines, lay dormant until a target was found and delete itself on 24 June 2012 no matter what to minimize exposure. Stuxnet was delivered through five companies related to the enrichment plants by infected USB sticks and used four Windows **zero-day exploits**, previously unknown security flaws that make malware likely to evade antivirus or firewall scans. Since each zero-day exploit would fetch a sizable sum on the black market and is enough to make devastating malware, it's plausible that Stuxnet creators weren't in it for the money *and* they wanted to make sure their malware did its job. When Stuxnet finally found the target is when things would start to spin out of control.

A target Siemens centrifuge would work just as expected most of the time but then would erratically spin up and slow down, which would cause it to gradually rip itself apart and have to be replaced. Stuxnet would also rig the reporting systems to show everything's fine, which would make any personnel on duty think they were just imagining things. Estimates by industrial analysts claim 200,000 computers may have been infected, 60% of them in Iran, and a grand total of 1,000 centrifuges were destroyed.

Stuxnet was detected by accident in 2010 when an Iranian nuclear power plant engineer noticed something weird on his work laptop that he brought home. The laptop was apparently infected by some malware as it was in a restart loop and nothing seemed to help; this would later turn out to be due to Stuxnet creators pushing out a botched update. A small security firm from Belarus took on the task and debunked the entire scheme, revealing that Stuxnet had been rampaging in Iran for at least two years. Kaspersky Labs, another security firm, delved deeper into Stuxnet[32] and discovered an astounding level of sophistication. It turned out that the makers of Stuxnet also managed to get ahold of two digital certificates used to sign software, meaning that Stuxnet was extremely resilient to scanning and appeared like a legitimate driver.

Stuxnet was apparently made by an entire unit of malware experts, estimated as having 22-30 people, as it utilized several programming languages and consisted of highly specialized modules, showing a great degree of understanding as to how a uranium enrichment plant works. Remember when we said customers buy software and never bother updating or buying a new version? Whoever made Stuxnet knew that Iranian nuclear enrichment plants were using outdated Windows machines, but the tragedy was Microsoft had patched quite a few of those vulnerabilities *in 2008;* Iranians simply never considered running an update.

Subsequent news reports, trickled statements from Israeli and US officials and books written about the incident[33] over the following years will favorably mention Stuxnet, praising it as a great

---

[32] https://www.infoworld.com/article/2626009/malware/is-stuxnet-the--best--malware-ever-.html

[33] https://arstechnica.com/tech-policy/2012/06/confirmed-us-israel-created-stuxnet-lost-control-of-it/

achievement and a part of Obama's cyber-war efforts called "Olympic Games". What nobody expected was for Stuxnet to get out into the wild. Just like we saw with the NSAkey debacle, software engineers often have no clue what they're working on, meaning that it's possible for a subgroup within a team to act of their own accord and hijack the code for whatever purposes they want, including sale on the black market or use in political mind games. Well, someone did modify Stuxnet code to create something even worse.

Duqu

Also known as "son of Stuxnet", Duqu is a 2011 trojan likely made by the same authors as it used similar code and also attacked Iran. Though researchers seem quite confident that's the case[34], do keep in mind that misdirection is a big part of cyber-warfare, and it's just as likely someone falsified data breadcrumbs to stoke antagonism between Israel, the US, and Iran. Remember what we said in the introduction of this book – be thoroughly paranoid when dealing with cybersecurity. In some sense, reality is much weirder than any kind of fiction, and we can't ever be completely certain who's telling the truth. Anyway, Duqu was not as discriminating as Stuxnet and could implant itself into any computer and any organization. Its end goal, however, remains unknown.

The name Duqu comes from the keylogger module that named the log files it generated DQ.TMP. Duqu spread through malicious Word documents that again exploited a zero-day to run arbitrary code with the highest administrator privileges. Authors used a **buffer overflow**, a strange behavior code that exhibits when faced with unusual data or requests. In general, well-written code would have a tightly defined range of acceptable data and strict responses to unusual inputs. For example, Windows built-in calculator should only deal with numbers and mathematical operators, so trying to load a JPEG file or a piece of Javascript code shouldn't work or would at worst

---

[34] https://arstechnica.com/information-technology/2011/10/spotted-in-iran-trojan-duqu-may-not-be-son-of-stuxnet-after-all/

crash the calculator. That is if the software engineers wrote the code right. If the program is left to decide what to do, then anything can happen, depending on how complex the program is.

Duqu used a buffer overflow in Word fonts, in particular, a font named "Dexter Regular". Details are scarce because of "security through obscurity", but in general the idea would be that a font can contain extra data that gives it visual flourish; a malicious font like this one would actually have *code* embedded in it. When WIN32K.SYS file, which in Windows is usually dedicated to processing graphical content and displaying it on a monitor or sending it to a printer, accesses this malicious font, the buffer overflow triggers. Since WIN32K.SYS has access to **kernel**, the core of a computer, it bypasses all checks and balances in order to maintain performance. That's when the code is executed, which lets the trojan be loaded into RAM with the highest administrator privileges. Meanwhile, the Word document is opened and may show a couple of pages with normal content. It's a pretty clever trick overall.

Duqu won't do anything but will keep track of keyboard and mouse activity until they cease for about ten minutes, after which it will start downloading additional modules. The first reported victims were actually cybersecurity firms that simulated hacking attacks against their own networks and discovered Duqu code. One theory[35] for Duqu's purpose is that it was *meant* to target security firms, such as those providing antivirus services, to compromise their products and steal digital certificates. However, Duqu could be equipped with a special module that would erase the victim's entire hard drive.

Duqu injected its process directly into RAM to minimize leaving files lying around and getting detected, but that also meant a machine restart would wipe it from the system. The keylogger part of Duqu could take screenshots and key presses on the infected machine, compress them in an archive and send them to a designated

---

[35] https://securelist.com/duqu-faq-33/32463/

email address. We saw that Turla hackers embedded video game references in their code but Duqu authors inserted a fragment of a JPEG file, an image captured through Hubble telescope that shows the gargantuan debris field of two galaxies smashing into one another millions of years ago.

At least 12 varieties of Duqu were discovered, each with its own configuration files and date ranges. It turned out authors would program Duqu to spy for up to 36 days and have it auto-destruct to minimize exposure. Dates inside configuration files showed that each victim had a specific Duqu variant prepared just for them right before the attack, which would point towards the authors having a vast library of malware at their disposal. Just when it seemed it couldn't get any worse, there was more weaponized malware discovered, again in Iran.

Flame/Skywiper

Flame was discovered in 2012 by an Iranian cybersecurity company in coordination with a Hungarian research lab that was hit by Duqu, calling it the most advanced malware ever discovered. Initially called Skywiper, Flame contained trojan, worm and keylogger capabilities and was able to record network traffic, audio, keystrokes, mouse clicks, Skype conversations and even hijack Bluetooth connections to siphon data off of any devices in the vicinity it can't infect. Both names were derived from files it used.

The vast majority of Flame's targets were in Iran, with initial estimates suggesting up to 1,000 infected machines across the Middle East, though the self-destruct mechanism inside Flame would indicate this number is much higher. Files for Flame rack up to 20MB, making it about 20 times larger than Stuxnet and at least 200 times more complicated; Flame is arguably the largest malware ever seen and analyzing it in its entirety could take up to ten years.

Flame scans the target machine to detect the presence of an anti-malware program and customizes its filenames and extensions to minimize the chances of detection. Flame authors were able to procure a fraudulent Microsoft digital signature that's commonly used to verify if the software is legitimate thanks to **hash collision**, a cryptographic attack that tries to find alternate solutions to some complicated math.

Imagine yourself running an email server where people can make an account. Each of your users chooses a username, which is the address, and a password. Email addresses are meant to be shared in public and can be stored on the email server in plaintext but how do you store passwords so nobody, not your employees, not hackers, not even you, can see them *and* so that they aren't exposed when someone tries to log in? The answer is by *hashing* them, which means taking a very complex mathematical formula that turns each character in a password into a hexadecimal number and then adds all those numbers together. So, when someone tries to log in, your hashing algorithm takes the password they presented, hashes it as well and compares to the hash in their account; if the two hashes match, it's the same password, and the user is granted entry.

If some burglar literally rips out and steals a hard drive from your email server with all the hashes of your users' passwords, not all is lost. It's impossible to reverse hashing, but the thief can now **brute force** hashes, essentially meaning he or she can do a dictionary attack with no pesky CAPTCHA until they find passwords one by one. In this case, hashing will help in that it will buy you time to do an investigation, maybe call the police and recover the hard drive before damage is done; users don't have to know about it. We'll see later how companies that experienced such catastrophic losses dealt with them.

There are two obvious problems to the idea of hashing. First, what happens if a user chooses a very short or a very simple password? *They shouldn't,* which is why companies plead with their users to use uppercase, lowercase, numbers and so on when choosing a password. The more complex the password, the more unique the hash, and because hackers have all the time in the world to keep randomly guessing passwords or using dictionary attacks, the simplest and shortest passwords will fall first. A solution to lazy users and weak passwords is to add **salt**, a random string of numbers that is unique to each password, as the password is being hashed.

Hold on, hashing and salting? Are we making scrambled eggs here? That's actually a pretty good analogy to what happens with hashing – we take data and scramble it in a way that it's impossible to get the original data back. So as far as describing some really heavy irreversible math, it goes a long way to explain what's happening in layman's terms. We haven't had access to any software engineer meetings where they discussed cryptography, but we can imagine they missed more than one lunch based on the number of food references in these terms.

XKCD made a funny comic dealing with password strength that tangentially relates to hashing[36], with the idea being that longer passwords using simple words are vastly stronger than short passwords using a jumbled mass of letters, numbers, and punctuation. Now, since that comic shows a very strong password and plenty of people think they're *so smart*, don't you dare use "correct horse battery staple" as your password; hackers have already added it to their dictionaries. In general, avoid entering your password *anywhere* other than on its login screen; for example, a hacker could post a clickbait headline "Passwords are being cracked, is your password safe?" and leave a form field. No matter what you enter, the result is programmed to assuage your fears, but the hacker is secretly recording all passwords to make a dictionary of his or her own.

Anyway, the second problem with hashing is that the hashing algorithm itself can be weak and tends to produce the same results for entirely different passwords, meaning the hashes *collide*. As computers advanced in strength, they made it easier to find collisions for older hashing algorithms, as what once took a decade to crack became a matter of seconds. That's *exactly* what happened with

---

[36] https://www.xkcd.com/936/

Flame and its hash collision attack on a Microsoft digital certificate that used an MD5 hashing algorithm.

Not just plaintext, but software can be hashed too, and that hash represents what's known as "digital signature" or "digital certificate". In this way, we can get a list of hashes from the software maker and ensure the files were the same as ordered and nobody tampered with them. In 1991, a hashing algorithm known as MD5 was made and it mostly focused on ensuring files weren't corrupted after a download; it was otherwise insecure for hashing. You can still find old websites, particularly ones that offer downloads, where MD5 hashes are shown so you can tell if the file is corrupted in some way after you downloaded it. However, MD5 was never meant to be used for signing certificates.

In 2008, security researchers actually used several Sony PlayStation 3 consoles working together to take a single MD5 certificate, do a hash collision attack and create brand new certificates that could appear legitimate. In 2013, Chinese students were able to find a collision to any given MD5 hash on an ordinary computer in under a second[37]. These should have been ample warning for Microsoft.

One version of a Microsoft server was still capable of creating digital certificates using MD5, and that's where Flame authors prodded and poked until they managed to create a fraudulent one that appeared legitimate, helping it avoid detection. The fake certificate was just one piece of the puzzle; Flame would essentially contain a complete suite of tools for cyber-espionage, focusing on PDF files, AutoCAD drawings, and text documents to hoover them off infected machines to one of 80 control servers around the globe.

Should you be worried?

Stuxnet, Duqu and Flame are legendary forms of malware that you're unlikely to ever encounter in your daily life. In fact, if a civilian spots them, it means something, somewhere, has gone horribly

---

[37] https://eprint.iacr.org/2013/170.pdf

wrong. The creator of all three is theorized to be **Equation Group**, a shadowy organization of hackers that dispenses hacking tools to anyone with a budget to match and isn't likely to go after ordinary random users. For us, the main source of danger stems from bad security habits, such as reusing passwords or making tons of needless accounts that increase attack surface. Still, it's good to know how malware operates as that reveals just how much pressure software companies face to deliver quality products.

The problem with cryptography and hashing, in general, is that once deployed, these algorithms stay still, but the computing power advances and makes it more likely the security of these measures will be breached. So, using older software becomes a gamble that's more and more likely to wipe you out as time goes on, but updating isn't always the best option since it costs money and disrupts your workflow. You don't have to feel obliged to update to the very last version of software as soon as it comes out − unless others are depending on you.

On the other hand, companies certainly should do as much as they can to tighten their cybersecurity efforts and stop data leaks, which are a frighteningly common occurrence. When your computer gets hacked, you can lose banking data but just as easily call the bank to reverse any given transaction; when Facebook gets hacked, millions of people will have their most intimate data, from chat conversations to photo albums exposed to hackers and possibly exploited at some point down the line.

Hospitals and airports are very vulnerable targets that we don't think about until they're hit with **ransomware**, malware that locks up the system until some money is paid to the hacker, usually cryptocurrency. In May 2017, WannaCry ransomware hit over 200 thousand computers across the world, including those in hospitals, banks, and airports. Some of these institutions used Windows XP way past its support date, making it trivial for hackers to waltz into an office, plug in an infected USB and lock down their entire network. Who made WannaCry? It was supposedly a hacking tool made by the NSA, stolen by a hacker group and repurposed for theft.

In any case, hardware and software failures *will* happen; hence, the smartest move is to back up your data, which is the only surefire way to protect against hacking. Separate the original and the backup as much as possible, preferably by having one on the cloud and the other on an external hard drive that's disconnected from the internet. Include photographs, voice messages and other personal trivia in your backup, so these precious memories don't get lost due to a hack.

Chapter 11 – Corporate Risk Assessment

In 2016, Yahoo reported that 500 million of its user accounts were hacked, with information such as names, addresses, phone numbers, MD5-hashed passwords and security questions exposed to hackers. That breach was separate from a 2013 hack, where *one billion* user accounts were exposed[38]. Also, there was another hack in 2014 – at this point, we can confidently state anyone with a Yahoo account had it hacked and if the account was tied to some other service that too might have been breached. We only learned about it years later[39] because Yahoo was in the process of being acquired by Verizon and any bad press would tank the price. How could this happen? Why were they using MD5, of all things? *What were they thinking?*

---

[38] https://www.wired.com/2016/12/yahoo-hack-billion-users/

[39] https://www.cnet.com/news/yahoo-announces-all-3-billion-accounts-hit-in-2013-breach/

We mentioned that ad companies track users online to make sophisticated psychological profiles. There's a lot of money to be made if behavior patterns can be elucidated and it's really nothing personal – it's just business. All companies end up exploiting user trust to make money, and these practices get worse as the company grows – it's just that those dishing out advertisements have the most egregious business practices.

Companies past a certain size can't afford to care about you as a person, but rather only see your characteristics in aggregate, as belonging to a demographic. So, in true hacker fashion, the same way these company executives analyze us, we're going to analyze *them*. Without revealing any personal information or anything like that, we'll delve into the managerial mindset to see the thought processes that led to some of the most devastating tech company hacks in recent history.

Imagine an itsy-bitsy animal, like an ant. For its size, one ant is surprisingly strong and can lift 50 times its weight because of how compact all of its parts are. However, what would happen if we enlarged an ant by, let's say, a factor of a thousand? Well, this small, gracious and impressive insect would essentially be useless and unable to move, immediately imploding on itself. It turns out that *not all concepts can scale*, meaning an ant is perfectly built for a creature the size of a few millimeters but anything larger than that simply doesn't work – a larger body requires larger muscles, which now need more energy, bigger digestion, stronger jaws and so on. A small ant is a great and versatile worker, but putting it in unnatural circumstances can only produce bad results; such an ant would also be an easy target for all sorts of predators. Unsustainable scaling is exactly at the core of what's plaguing all tech companies, at least ones that get hit by hacking attacks.

When a tech company starts out, it's usually driven by an enthusiast with passion and a vision who understands one highly specific problem, such as the lack of ways to cheaply and instantly communicate with people we hold dear; hence, we got social networks. The enthusiast then pours his heart and soul into the company to make his idea a reality, stabilize company revenue and nurse it to profitability. Overtime is a must, and everyone's performing a dozen roles at once to save money. If the company survives this tumultuous period, which most don't, it eventually attracts the attention of business investors, who are now ready to inject cash streams into the company and make it become even bigger, but there's a catch – the company must now become managed rather than led.

The owner can sit back, relax and enjoy the fruits of his labor as managers swarm in, each of which has an impressive resume but little, if any, hands-on experience with the niche. Whereas before the company was a tightly-knit group of people that kept it lean and trimmed, these managers don't really do much of anything or even understand how the underlying technology works and yet have a say in how things are done. So, they schedule meetings, send out memos and regulate office life down to the tiniest detail, focusing on spreadsheets and data-driven reports rather than hands-on experience.

As the company grows, managerial types are drawn to it like barnacles to an anchored ship. According to the **Peter Principle**[40], all managers *fail upwards* and settle in a position where their skills simply make them average rather than outstanding. This process is irreversible and results in the company slowly losing touch with reality, customers, and the market, becoming just a shadow of itself. Those who do actual productive work become a minority and managers get to rule with their firm handshakes, confident eye contact, and PowerPoint presentations. If you've ever felt frustrated by the actions of a company you previously cherished, it was likely because managers got ahold of the helm and are running the ship into the ground.

---

[40] https://www.investopedia.com/terms/p/peter-principle.asp

When customers start abandoning ship, managers will try to toss the excess weight overboard, which usually means firing the most rebellious workers until those remaining learn to become yes-men, essentially starting to mimic managers to survive. Replacements cycle through the company, get paid peanuts and leave an even greater mess until their job positions get outsourced. When the company is no longer growing, management buys a promising new startup or just any related company to shuffle a few managers around and maintain the appearance of growth. None of this is meant to hurt the company; if anything, managers usually have honest intentions and just want everyone to get along.

Dictionary of Managerial Jargon[41] shows some common phrases used by managers, such as "our profits are better than expected", that are meant to generate agreement by using evasive and vague words. By never really committing with any given statement, a manager can never be caught in a lie or made accountable, no matter what happens, which protects the company from lawsuits. Empty phrases, feel-good statements, and circular logic abound in any manager statement, especially when that manager is put in the hot seat and wants to keep his job.

Managers also have two duties: one of caring for their customers and the other of increasing company value. They can both be fulfilled if the managers were to understand what the customers want and why, but that's rarely the case. The problem is that company value can be quantified as revenue growth, but customer care is intangible and comprises of things such as goodwill and product quality; managers get promotions and raises for increased revenue but nothing for customers being happy with the product. So, managers tend towards *saying they care and acting like they don't*. All companies that survive in the market always end up the same way – managerial bloat that leads to gradual whittling of goodwill of customers and

---

[41] http://dictionaryofmanagementjargon.yolasite.com/

degradation of product quality. That's when the company is ripe for the hacking.

On 28 September 2018, Facebook announced 50 million user accounts were accessed by an unknown hacker or group of hackers[42]. He or she used a bug in Facebook's "View As" feature that normally allows any user to see their profile as another Facebook user. If you chose a friend who had someone in their friends list with a birthday on that day, Facebook would pop up a birthday celebration video *for you*, setting authentication tokens on your machine and allowing *you* to log in as the user you viewed Facebook as.

The problem was in shoddy implementation of the View As feature done to save time and money; it wasn't a distinct feature on Facebook but it basically temporarily logged you in as that user. This exploit also allowed the hackers access to *any website or service that could use a Facebook login as that user.* Sorry, did we say September 28? Hackers breached Facebook's security *11 days earlier* – the delay was the company trying to contain and measure the breach before reporting on it.

Guy Rosen, Facebook's VP of Product *Management*, had this to say in the press release concerning the matter[43]: "People's privacy and security is incredibly important, and we're sorry this happened." That doesn't really change anything, but it makes the customers feel they're taken care of by a company with revenue of $13.5 billion in the third quarter of 2018 alone[44], almost all of it from advertising. It's a really neat idea for a service – expose the hidden advertisement

---

[42] https://www.forbes.com/sites/thomasbrewster/2018/09/29/how-facebook-was-hacked-and-why-its-a-disaster-for-internet-security/#640867e42033

[43] https://newsroom.fb.com/news/2018/09/security-update/

[44] https://investor.fb.com/investor-news/press-release-details/2018/Facebook-Reports-Third-Quarter-2018-Results/default.aspx

profile to users and have them *fill it out for you* to be then sold piecemeal for advertising purposes.

In December 2017, Facebook decided to remove a feature termed "disputed flag". The idea was that many users were visiting Facebook to get news but were eschewing mainstream news sources in favor of minnow websites that often produced **clickbait**, misleading headlines with the sole purpose of pumping up traffic stats. Facebook attempted to steer users away from such news articles by placing a bright, bold warning icon next to them; it turned out users were actually *more likely* to read such articles. Remember what we said about banner blindness? Users scan content with peripheral vision and the disputed flag turned out to be a powerful magnet for attention, in a sense serving as Facebook's seal of approval. You, dear reader, might not know the first thing about running a billion-dollar company, but by simply reading this book, you've learned a few simple and basic cybersecurity principles; in contrast, the people in charge of Facebook are *blithering idiots*.

TESSA LYONS, PRODUCT MANAGER at Facebook, had this to say[45] about disputed flags: "Academic research on correcting misinformation has shown that putting a strong image, like a red flag, next to an article may actually entrench deeply held beliefs – the opposite effect to what we intended." Why were disputed flags introduced if they weren't supported by science? It truly is a clown parade.

In response to massive hacks and persistent clickbait plaguing Facebook, Mark Zuckerberg pledged[46] to renew efforts in keeping the platform clean while warning that it might not be enough. In his own words, "These are not problems that we fix." He has a cold, smart and straightforward approach to Facebook hacks. They won't

---

[45] https://newsroom.fb.com/news/2017/12/news-feed-fyi-updates-in-our-fight-against-misinformation/

[46] https://www.businessinsider.com/facebook-warns-security-and-safety-costs-will-rise-in-2019-2018-10

be stopped; they will be *managed*. Stopping hacks would cost money but managing them only takes a few press releases and an appearance in front of the Congress to give non-answers. As long as users keep coming back, Facebook will keep raking in the cash.

Consider the frightening concept of Facebook managing what the users can see and read, purging what's deemed unacceptable from the platform rather than letting users choose for themselves. This actually defeats the entire concept of a social network where users can freely share and interact with one another. In September 2018, Facebook announced new ways of automatically discovering clickbait by using machine learning, a set of software that can learn from patterns and context. Antonia Woodford, Facebook's Product *Manager*, had this to say in a press release[47], "We know that people want to see accurate information on Facebook, so for the last two years, we've made fighting misinformation a priority." Thanks to this crusade against clickbait, a whole gaggle of managers will get to justify their salaries, hire fact-checkers, write more reports, pat themselves on the back and overall feel like they've done something productive.

Even when the company does the best it can to safeguard against hacks, it can still get hit. In 2010, Google was hit by a massive hack attack apparently originating from China, dubbed Operation Aurora[48]. Internet Explorer zero-day exploit was used to install encrypted malware to avoid detection, open a backdoor and siphon off intellectual property. 34 companies in total were hit.

From the above, it's clear that there's no safe way to use certain websites and services. The concept of social media itself is unsustainable, Facebook's low and mid-level management has no clue what it's doing, and people at the top know hacks are unavoidable but still press on. Get off any social media right this

---

[47] https://newsroom.fb.com/news/2018/09/expanding-fact-checking/

[48] https://www.wired.com/2010/01/operation-aurora/

instant; they're a cybersecurity nightmare. If you have to share anything online, never post truthful information or just record a voice message using a smartphone and send it as an email attachment to your friends and family.

As a conscious customer and someone interested in cybersecurity, it is your task to associate with and support companies that do honest business using solid security practices rather than decrepit tech giants that leak or *sell* your private data. Better yet, start a tech company of your own and show the world how it's done. Decentralization is exactly what the tech world needs to create a safe cyber-space; a few tech giants are simply too big of a target.

Chapter 12 – Cryptocurrencies and Mesh Routing

Imagine having an idling car in a garage. By letting the car idle, you spend gasoline, but also get a chance to capture some smoke. This is because there is a niche market of smoke enthusiasts, who also gather and resell smoke to one another. There's no rhyme or reason why they're doing it or why the price of any given type of smoke is the way it is. You do manage to make some money selling smoke, but it barely covers the cost of gasoline. Your dream is to get just the right kind of smoke that will have its price suddenly shoot to the moon so you can sell it for millions and buy yourself a Lamborghini. Meanwhile, the gasoline prices spike, there is extra pollution being made for no reason, neighbors are complaining about the noise, heat, and smoke are coming out of your garage, and now the tax authority wants to look into your smoke shenanigans. Makes no sense? Then it's a perfect analogy for cryptocurrencies.

Bitcoin, created by the mythical Satoshi Nakamoto, is a series of hash solutions to some needlessly complicated math that gets harder as time goes on. Hashes are combined by miners into blocks that get added to an immutable, append-only public ledger called blockchain that each node should be able to have for transparency. Having a publicly verifiable, cryptographically secure and trustless currency made all breeds of anarchists jump right in for the greater good and start mining Bitcoin for their own selfish needs. The very first Bitcoin block contains a text message: *The Times 03/Jan/2009 Chancellor on brink of second bailout for banks*, placed there by Satoshi[49], who also mined about a million Bitcoin for himself, worth $6.5 billion as of November 2018.

Nobody could determine the real identity of "Satoshi" or even if he's a real person; he was either a genius, a group of hackers or an intelligence agency working for some inexplicable goal. There's nothing special about Bitcoin since anyone can create their own fork using open source code, and indeed, today there are thousands of different digital coins that also hold no real value or utility.

Cryptocurrencies are crawling with scammers and criminals looking to launder money or purchase illegal substances. All transactions are public and managing wallets is a nightmare, nudging users into leaving their cryptocurrency on exchanges that are regularly "hacked". The most notorious example of this is **Mt. Gox**, an exchange that initially dealt with Magic the Gathering cards. In 2014, Mt. Gox lost $460 million in Bitcoin, and the whole thing might have as well been an inside job[50], seeing how poorly the exchange was coded. Users learned absolutely nothing out of it – those that weren't wiped out transferred their funds to other exchanges and just kept going.

---

[49] https://en.bitcoin.it/wiki/Genesis_block

[50] https://www.wired.com/2014/03/bitcoin-exchange/

Trying to mine cryptocurrency is fruitless as the Chinese have a chokehold on both the technology and mining speed, being able to control the market volume and manipulate the prices as they please. Worse yet, tax authorities have started requiring cryptocurrency profits be reported and in some cases taxed, regardless if the person actually cashed any of it out. Don't get involved.

What started as an anarcho-hacker experiment in creating a new currency actually showed some interesting trends relevant to cybersecurity. As Bitcoin difficulty increases, the weakest miners drop off, and the remaining ones pool their hash power together, meaning that *power inevitably centralizes*. Blockchain contains a record of all Bitcoin transactions ever made and currently stands at over 200GB and steadily increasing, with few miners being capable and willing to read it. Users readily accepted this deviation from the original decentralized Bitcoin design, showing that *users are too trusting*. So, centralized entities with immense power that check transactions, produce currency and are trusted by users – that sounds an awful lot like banks but without checks and security features that currently exist in banking. Every hack attack we've covered so far can be said to arise from either or both of those innate vulnerabilities that have to do with how humans use technology rather than the technology itself.

Bitcoin miners eventually recognized the need for scalability and fee-less micropayments, proposing a temporary Lightning Network, calling it 'the internet of money'. Under Lightning Network, every Bitcoin holder would serve as a node and connect to other nearest nodes, eschewing blockchain altogether. Sounds good but cryptocurrency developers regularly present vague concepts that have not a sliver of hope of working in the next century. For example, the Lightning Network whitepaper[51] says Bitcoin "delivery may be lossy, similar to packets on the internet." It sounds so easy

---

[51] https://lightning.network/lightning-network-paper.pdf

when put like that, but how does the internet work? Is it really trustless and decentralized, as Satoshi preached Bitcoin should be?

As explained by Rick Falkvinge, the leader of Swedish Pirate Party, "Mesh routing is an unsolved problem."[52] The only way the internet packets can go from Berlin to San Francisco in a fraction of a second is due to a **Border Gateway Protocol**, an agreement between handlers of internet traffic to play nice. There are no adversaries at the ISP level, and the only reason why we can use the internet at all is because these business people have made a pinky swear always to be honest about delivering internet traffic where it belongs. The same ways kids on the playground reach a set of rules and keep to them, ISPs shoulder a gargantuan volume of internet traffic with nothing more than mutual understanding. It truly boggles the mind, doesn't it?

When you want to visit, say, a Russian website, your ISP takes your request and advertises it to all the other ISPs, "Hey, I've got a user who wants to visit this IP, who's going to take it?" and an ISP that can fulfill the request volunteers for it, bringing you to the website. There are no hash checks, no cryptography or anything like that to ensure compliance but simply a code of honor and the fact any misbehaving ISPs will get cut off by all the others, tanking the value of their infrastructure. Adversaries can get introduced at the ISP level too, and that's when everyone starts feeling queasy.

In April 2017, chunks of internet traffic were mysteriously rerouted[53] to go through a Russian ISP. Accidental rerouting can happen at times, but the chunks are indiscriminate and usually consist of both individual and company traffic. In this case, however, the traffic was exclusively related to banking, consisting of VISA, Mastercard and similar transaction data over the course of six-seven minutes. After

---

[52] https://youtu.be/DFZOrtlQXWc?t=578

[53] https://arstechnica.com/information-technology/2017/04/russian-controlled-telecom-hijacks-financial-services-internet-traffic/

the hijacking ended, the ISP resumed its normal operation. Something similar happened on nine occasions in 2013, but the traffic was routed through Belarus and Icelandic ISPs before being sent to its destination.

One important factor that makes all the ISPs play nice is that they're all in a position of equal power, meaning they can *reciprocate*. Any given ISP holds total dominion over its users and can leverage their numbers as a bargaining chip when negotiating with other ISPs. This is unlike anything else that exists online, and no other website or service works like that, but maybe they should.

When you sign up for a Facebook or Twitter account, you're put in an unequivocal position of subservience – the company gets to dictate the terms and you can either take it or leave it. You have nothing to negotiate with, and terms favor the company, usually giving it plenty of leeway to abuse whatever discretion it has. The sickest perversion is that terms of use can change at a moment's notice and you're supposed to simply drop everything you've done so far and walk away if you disagree. Compare this to signing a contract with strictly defined terms that aren't meant to change. In conclusion, we might have to organize into groups and sign access contracts with online services to finally gain the respect we deserve and bargaining power we need to raise the level of cybersecurity to where hacks don't happen, or the services we use are made to pay us for lapses.

Chapter 13 – Card Transaction Security

Hackers steal card information too, sometimes by installing ATM skimmers that go over the card slot and read the data as it's being fed to the system[54]. It pays to be paranoid and constantly observe the environment for unusual details, in this case, video traces of glue holding the skimmer in place, which allowed the narrator to spot the skimmer. In 2012, a Dominican gang used ATM skimmers or a similar method to access 1.5 million card details[55]. When the news broke, the official statement by Mastercard was, in part, "MasterCard is concerned whenever there is any possibility that cardholders could be inconvenienced." Hold on, that's it? Inconvenience? Why aren't they worried?

Skimming is all the hacker can do because the card architecture is locked down tighter than Fort Knox. The card itself is just a piece of

---

[54] https://www.youtube.com/watch?v=ll4f0Wim4pM

[55] https://www.dailymail.co.uk/news/article-2123854/1-5million-account-numbers-hacked-Visa-Mastercard-card-data-theft.html

plastic with a bare bones magnetic strip and a chip, which costs the bank pennies to produce and allows issuance of as many cards as needed. There is a simple counter inside the chip that ticks up whenever the card is used. Bank servers supposedly keep a copy of this counter and trigger an alarm if there's a mismatch. Think about the implications – if someone does skim your card to create a perfectly functional copy, all you have to do is *use your card*. Your card's counter goes up by one, the bank servers synchronize, and you go on your merry way. When the hacker inserts his own copy, the counters no longer match, and the ATM simply refuses to return the fraudulent card.

If the user spots any odd transactions, he simply has to contact the bank within 30 days and ask for a refund. The bank cancels the old card, issues a new one at practically no cost and starts an investigation. The user can be called in to sign an affidavit attesting the transaction was fraudulent, so the bank can legally pursue him for attempted fraud if the investigation shows that's what happened. The destination bank is notified, and they do the same investigation on their end, settling the accounts when the truth is found out. All funds are insured anyway, so the bank might actually *make money* when someone steals from it.

Cards that have short-range RFID chip technology for contactless pay can apparently be abused as well thanks to some antenna handiwork. RFID uses radio waves that reach out six inches, so a hacker wearing a special antenna costing about $300 could bump into a victim and scoop up all the information from the card[56] through clothes. The defense to this kind of hacking – and it's not a joke – would be to wrap the card or the wallet in tin foil, but again the banking system has redundant layers of protection.

Paying with a card with or without RFID at the register requires the store to have a special merchant bank account that is secured and

---

[56] https://www.dailymail.co.uk/sciencetech/article-2948212/Will-victim-digital-pickpockets-Hacker-reveals-easy- steal-credit-card-numbers-air-SECONDS.html

insured against theft. As soon as a customer complains about odd transactions, the thief will be spotted through security cameras, transactions reversed and the merchant put on notice; too many thefts and the merchant account is fined or shut down. Card transactions are secured with layers upon layers of such unobtrusive security, each of them being cheap, robust and lightweight. For example, an ATM has a minimalistic keyboard to reduce the chances of a buffer overflow through special characters that could give a user access to **firmware**, code embedded in the hardware.

What's surprising is that cards work, but cryptocurrencies don't when it should be the other way around. Cryptocurrencies are shielded with military-grade impenetrable math, and yet an irreversible Bitcoin transaction may take two months to complete with medium to high fees; a card transaction basically works on goodwill and yet is instant, reversible and has no fees. What this can teach us is that *technology is only as trustworthy as the environment it's deployed in.* Cryptocurrencies presume everyone participating is an adversary, but card issuers presume the cardholder is trusted until proven otherwise; that's what makes a world of difference.

It's impossible to deploy any kind of digital technology in a hostile environment and then bend ourselves backward to stop adversaries from using it while keeping all the benefits of that technology – security measures inevitably frustrate and degrade usability for legitimate users. Relying strictly on technology will never work in establishing cybersecurity; people delegate authority anyway and instinctively seek someone to trust, so they'll *give* power to someone to fix problems, which again raises questions of potential abuse. How does one entrust companies with things such as **biometric data**, the essential descriptions of our body, without them being stolen?

Card structure actually combines three major defense layers: authenticator, password and biometric data. You never realized it, but using a card means having a physical token, which is the card; knowing a password, which is the PIN and matching biometric data, which is the signature. Each of these is basic and easily defeated, but when combined, they present a solid defense against hacking with minimal hassle and intrusion. Just imagine giving your fingerprints or having your eye scanned when signing up for a card; it's enough to make even the most devout cybersecurity zealot quiver a bit, but giving out a signature is even kind of fun. *That's the kind of cybersecurity we need.* Any kind of cybersecurity system of the future should look up to how banks have done it and copy it as much as possible.

Do be careful when researching card security – banks have absolutely no sense of humor when it comes to technology their livelihood depends on and wield legal, economic and media power to shut down any research attempts.

Chapter 14 – Cryptojacking

Hackers warmed up to the idea of cryptocurrency-mining malware as a way to steal money through the victim's power bill. By visiting a website, the hapless user gets Javascript code that keeps running in the browser and mines cryptocurrency for the hacker. The user only notices a huge spike in memory, CPU and GPU usage while on the page that may cause components to draw more power. There is also a lot of heat generated during cryptocurrency mining, which can cause the machine to catch fire. In one case in Siberia, an entire apartment went up in flames thanks to a mining setup by one occupant[57]. In Brooklyn in February 2018, T-Mobile complained about radio interference to FCC, who found a cluster of Bitcoin miners that were running as such speeds that they created radio signals[58]. Since **cryptojacking**, stealthy loading, and execution of a cryptocurrency miner doesn't steal any data, victims often feel no need to report or pursue hackers, who can thus get a fraction of a cent from each infected machine a day with no risk.

---

[57]http://www.siberiantimes.com/other/others/news/cryptocurrency-goes-up-in-smoke-fire-caused-by-bitcoin-mining/

[58] https://www.reuters.com/article/us-crypto-currencies-fcc/u-s-probe-finds-bitcoin-mining-operation-interfered-with-broadband-network-idUSKCN1FZ321

Crypto miners found on websites can be willingly placed there by the website or injected through an XSS exploit, but classical crypto miner malware that infects the desktop exists as well. Antiviruses and firewalls still struggle to detect crypto malware, but the best indicator of such activity would be sending out more traffic than what's received. In November 2017, some 33,000 websites with a combined traffic of a billion monthly users were found to run crypto miners, and 40% of most common malware in 2018 were also crypto miners[59].

In an ironic case of "no honor among thieves", some crypto malware will come with a list of competitor miners and code to remove them from the infected system[60] before installing itself. Another flavor of crypto malware hijacks the copy/paste function of the operating system to affect clipboard contents. When a user copy/pastes addresses in his wallet to send cryptocurrencies, the malware triggers and injects preset addresses that belong to the hacker in a blink of an eye.

Turning off Javascript in the browser stops crypto miners dead in their tracks but also makes plenty of websites unusable. See how it works? When Javascript was first deployed, it opened up a whole new world of possibilities, but now we're stuck with using this outdated layer of technology that first became a nuisance, then a mandate and then an attack vector. If you were to turn off cookies and Javascript, both of which were designed to be *choices* rather than mandates, you'd essentially be cut off from using the internet despite having perfectly functioning hardware and software.

---

[59] https://www.csoonline.com/article/3253572/internet/what-is-cryptojacking-how-to-prevent-detect-and-recover-from-it.html

[60]

https://www.comodo.com/GTR/Q2/2018/ComodoCybersecurityGlobalThreatReportQ22018Edition.pdf

Chapter 15 – The Internet of Things

The 'Internet of Things' (IoT) represents the latest catchphrase that's meant to make you consume more than ever, buying accessories simply because they were designed as a part of a loosely connected mesh. IoT opens a whole new world of possibilities and, of course, it's merely a choice. Google's Nest Home System[61] is one such consumer solution that envelops an abode in a veil of security. Nest Guard is the size of half an orange that sits on the table and is used to tap in using Nest Tag, a small doohickey that looks like a round cotton pad. Nest Detect is a stick that can be set near windows and doors to detect opening or movement and finally the Nest App on a smartphone coordinates between them. Additional products include thermostats, locks and smoke detectors.

There's a possibility of adding a password, so Nest Home System combines authenticator and password approaches but has no biometric data capability. Another problem is that the inner workings of Nest products are accessible by simply poking and prodding; by having no security through obscurity, the system's flaws become

---

[61] https://nest.com/alarm-system/overview/

obvious to anyone who looks. The worst part? It's connected to the internet.

IoT connectivity is touted as enabling constant access to the status of the Nest Home System, but that feature handily defeats the entire purpose of the product – a home security system is *meant* to work without the owner looking at it all the time. Internet access means hackers from China, Zimbabwe or Burundi can access Nest products just as easily as the owner and do with them as they please. Devices with internet connectivity, such as cameras and thermometers, can also undergo cryptojacking. It's here that we finally discover just how devastating a hack attack can be when everything is connected to the internet.

White hat group known as LMG has successfully cryptojacked[62] a best-seller wireless camera on Amazon, TENVIS HD. Opening up the camera and hooking up their own hardware to it showed a password-protected admin account. A brute force approach cracked the password in 15 seconds; it was eight zeroes. The camera was then made a part of **botnet**, a collection of hijacked devices that can perform DoS attacks or mine cryptocurrency. One such IoT botnet, called Mirai, first showed up in 2016, when hackers operating it simply scanned a huge swath of internet ports for IoT devices and tried dictionary attacks, hijacking many of them in the process[63]. Mirai botnet was then used to temporarily shut down the internet on the East Coast in October 2016[64].

LMG ordered the camera to download the mining code and hijacked the camera's processor, running it at 200%. Network traffic scans show regular spikes in network traffic as the camera receives orders

---

[62] https://lmgsecurity.com/cryptojacking-meets-iot/

[63] https://www.csoonline.com/article/3258748/security/the-mirai-botnet-explained-how-teen-scammers-and-cctv-cameras-almost-brought-down-the-internet.html

[64] https://www.wired.com/2016/10/internet-outage-ddos-dns-dyn/

and sends out cryptocurrency that should be detected by a wary owner, but most IoT devices are never examined past installation. By 2020, there will be an estimated 30 billion IoT devices in the world.

The main problem with IoT devices is the default username and password combination that most users never change. In general, users in the cyberspace will use defaults most of the time, even when it's to their detriment. If you're intent on trying out IoT, use a device or program that can sniff out their network traffic, and do change the password as instructed in the Flame/Skywiper chapter.

Chapter 16 – Russian Bots

After the 2016 US presidential election, mainstream media outlets experienced a major case of sour grapes, blaming Donald Trump's victory on Russian bots. How exactly did Russian bots influence the election is never quite explained, but the narrative appears to consist of simply repeating the phrase "Russian bots" over and over again without context. In one 2017 *The New York Times* article[65], we get a picture of a fake Facebook account that supposedly acted as a Russian bot, lashing out against Democrats to stoke resentment.

The article doesn't investigate the reach this account had, but based on the image in the article that shows one of its posts, the fake account had a grand total of *one* like on it, which could have been the bot itself. We've previously established that Facebook is reluctant to delete user accounts as they fatten up their user stats, but after the Russian bots' narrative, Facebook started deleting roughly a million

---

[65] https://www.nytimes.com/2017/09/07/us/politics/russia-facebook-twitter-election.html

accounts *a day*, likely hitting many legitimate Russophile users in the process. Twitter initially allowed bots but also buckled under pressure from the mainstream media to start purging accounts.

Bots online would rather be used to create a fake following, catapulting someone into the media stratosphere. Let's imagine Rick wanting to sell his products through Twitter. Rick would otherwise have to painstakingly build his account for years on end before gaining a foothold; Rick can also simply contact a third-party Twitter botnet owner to buy in the ballpark of 100 thousand likes and retweets for a couple of hundred dollars. It's not only easy, but it's laughably easy and cheap. Of course, if Rick makes 50 tweets and only one gets that kind of attention, the users will notice something fishy and debunk him, but the point is that social media exploit our inherent desire for social proof, one of the principles of social engineering. We *want* to know what everyone else is thinking and be involved in the coolest new thing.

Never trust the publicly displayed metrics, such as the number of likes, dislikes, views, upvotes and so on. These are simply numbers in a database anyone with an admin access can edit as he or she pleases. In a most recent example from November 2018, a video game studio Activision-Blizzard announced a mobile spinoff of a popular franchise, Diablo. The fans were furious and bombed the Youtube announcement videos with nearly half a million dislikes, but the dislike count kept dropping by a hundred thousand at a time[66]. Google can always hide behind the "it's the bots disliking and we simply removed them" but the problem is there's no transparency in either the upvoting or downvoting process on any of these platforms, let alone when it comes to vote removal and account banning processes.

Accusations of Russian bots interfering in US politics have made the political discussion even more toxic than usual – since there's no

---

[66] https://www.ubergizmo.com/2018/11/dislikes-are-disappearing-from-diablo-immortals-youtube-trailer/

way to *prove or disprove* any of them. It's the ultimate exercise in solipsism, arrogant belief that only the speaker is real and everyone else is a figment of his imagination. As we've discussed previously, Alan Turing devised a machine that could mimic human chatting behavior in the 1950s, and there hasn't been any headway on countering it since. There is simply no way to know if any content made online is produced by a bot or a human, which means we should judge all content based on its merit rather than the originator's intent or association. If bots can produce better content than humans, then they should be embraced regardless of who runs them and for what purpose. This doesn't mean bots don't exist online, but they're not necessarily Russian, and they don't necessarily want to interfere in the presidential elections.

Just like we saw with Stuxnet, nation-sponsored bots and malware would try to *avoid* detection by *hiding* from humans, not interacting with them. When bots or malware want to communicate in public, it would be done in a way that goes unnoticed, as was the case with one malicious Firefox plugin. In 2017, ESET security researchers discovered[67] one such plugin was fetching its orders by visiting Britney Spears' Instagram photos and combing through comments until a special one was found. The plugin would hash each comment until it found one that hashed to 183, and then inserted that comment into a special formula to extract a web address where the Turla command server lay in wait.

The comment itself was completely ordinary, except that it had a few weird hashtags and typos but otherwise could have just as well been a regular user typing on a phone keyboard in a hurry. You would never notice this kind of comment or think it strange – since everyone's hopping from one page to the next in search of amazing content. So, try to be as precise as possible to eliminate doubt as to whether you're a bot or not and try to create content that stands on its

[67] https://www.welivesecurity.com/2017/06/06/turlas-watering-hole-campaign-updated-firefox-extension-abusing-instagram/

own merit rather than simply sharing what's upvoted, retweeted or liked.

Don't accuse anyone of being a bot. Some bots can be operated by humans so the bot account could change behavior on a dime. The very accusation of being a bot is very dehumanizing, so only make it in private to the website owner; don't say it in public. There are online services that gauge Twitter account's behavior to tell you if it's a bot[68]. Use them before throwing accusations.

---

[68] https://www.howtogeek.com/325232/how-to-check-if-a-twitter-account-is-a-bot/

Chapter 17 – Edward Snowden

When our presence online mostly consists of giving out private and metadata like free candy on Halloween, it's only a matter of time before government agencies decide to scoop it all up. In 2013, the UK's *The Guardian* published a series of blockbuster stories of a US whistleblower who had access to the NSA's government programs that spied on *everyone* indiscriminately. The first story revolved around a US phone operator, Verizon, giving the NSA unfettered access to *all* phone records of *all* its customers. 24 hours later, another blockbuster fell as a secret NSA program called **PRISM** was revealed.

The Verizon story was just an introduction to the concept of PRISM, that being that the NSA has full access to servers of companies such as Google, Yahoo, Facebook, and others. You can imagine how it works: the NSA issues a request to the company and threatens shutdown due to "national security" if the company refuses. No media will cover such a story, again due to national security, and court orders, if any, will also be sealed. In this way, every company that values the privacy of its customers gets quietly weeded out of the market, and only the compliant ones are left to succeed. If a tech company is successful, consider it an extension of the government surveillance apparatus; there's simply no way around it.

Looking at things from the perspective of the NSA, a tech company can't be allowed to operate where it can jeopardize national interests. The story gets repeated over and over again in cybersecurity – users are too trusting with whom they give authority, and the power centralizes, leading to abuses. There is no known solution to controlling international company behavior while respecting the right of citizens to privacy. What the NSA is doing is the best they could think of, and they just went with it as far as it possibly could. As we've seen with CFAA, legislators don't have the first clue about technology and just give a blank check to surveillance agencies. That's how we ended up with PRISM.

A few days later, the whistleblower outed himself as Edward Snowden, a former NSA employee, now in exile in Russia. The stories will keep coming out[69], each more devastating than the previous. Heads of governments were also under NSA surveillance, even those that were considered allies. XKeyscore, an NSA program that allows a complete overview of any person's online existence, was also revealed by Snowden.

Its operation is shown in the 2016 movie *Snowden*: an NSA operator sits at a keyboard and logs into the target's Facebook account, having complete access and search capability. The operator can look through chats, images, and videos, cross-reference them with the rest of the user's online existence and do as they please, all without leaving any trace of activity. Evidence can be planted if need be, and there's nobody the user can appeal to, as it all seems legitimate. However, if the user would just do a simple favor to the NSA, the evidence would disappear just as easily as it came into being.

---

[69] https://mashable.com/2014/06/05/edward-snowden-revelations/

The NSA invested great efforts to crack encryption methods and infiltrate tech companies and links between them. In a true cloak-and-dagger fashion, the NSA trusts nobody and will both demand access to company servers and secretly tap into the lines to make sure it's all being scooped up. SMS messages are collected too, around 200 million each day. All this data is stored in one of the NSA's facilities strewn across the country, such as the $1.7 billion one in Utah[70] that spans 1 million square feet. State officials were supportive of the facility, as they got federal funding for certain projects, and besides, they have nothing to hide.

What Snowden revealed was a comprehensive hacking attempt, this time by a government agency with access to taxpayer funds. Every device that has electronics is hackable, and the NSA probably hacked it ten years ago. All digital communication efforts can and are being intercepted for the matters of national security. The main point is to realize that electronics are inherently insecure. Government agencies can mandate backdoors in software and even hardware, and there's nothing we can do except try to use open source as much as possible. Nothing is sacred, and there's no escape from the tyranny of surveillance, but we can make the task harder for hackers.

We should also try to *understand* electronics and systems before starting to use them. Electronic devices we're using have plenty of unused functions that have no business being there, such as front-facing cameras in smartphones, supposedly to take selfies. What Snowden does is rip a smartphone open, take out the cameras and the microphone, and plug in headphones when he has to make a call. When unused, disconnect the devices from the internet or simply monitor them for strange signs that could indicate hacking attempts.

---

[70] https://www.theguardian.com/world/2013/jun/14/nsa-utah-data-facility

Chapter 18 – Smartphones

When Snowden first met Guardian's reporters, he actually asked them to turn off their phones, take out the batteries and put both in the fridge, which should act as a Faraday cage to block radio waves. This would imply a smartphone is a listening device at all times, even when the battery is out. Well, a microwave is probably a much better choice than a fridge[71]. Everyone has a smartphone, and they seem like the perfect pocket assistant, providing entertainment and increasing productivity. We carry them everywhere, but they're a massive attack vector.

Google's Android is an open-source smartphone operating system with some proprietary components. This makes it open to hackers, with almost all mobile malware targeting Android. Even though apps for Android are meant to come exclusively through the Google Play Store, which should review all code, sometimes a few slip by. In

[71] https://mentalfloss.com/article/51597/does-refrigerator-make-good-faraday-cage

October 2018, a security researcher found malware disguised as banking, cleaning and coupon apps on Google Play Store[72]. To lower exposure, hackers only offered these apps to Brazilian users. Once installed, the app would request the user allow accessibility services for the app, which would let it read sensitive data, such as usernames and passwords.

Other apps secretly use the microphone and cameras to spy on the user, all with his or her permission. Facebook's Messenger app is probably the most notorious example, asking permission to access: identity, contacts, location, SMS, call diary, files and images, cameras, microphone, and Wi-Fi connection information. When allowed, the app will feed all that data to Facebook's servers to create a hidden profile for the user that fills out gaps in his actual Facebook profile. So, the app will cross-reference your phone numbers with existing Facebook users, then find and recommend those people to you. The app can also know if you spent the night at a friend's place by scanning nearby Wi-Fi networks and even know if you're going on foot by triangulating the strengths of nearby Wi-Fi signals. All social media apps look for a similar level of access and all for the same reason – spying on the user.

IOS is Apple's closed source operating system powering iPhones, with a major update released each year. The security of iPhones is solid[73], with a co-processor known as Secure Enclave at its core running Touch ID to read user's fingerprints, Face ID for facial scans and password storage. Breaking through Secure Enclave would likely require a $200,000 workstation with an electron microscope and micron-sized needles to punch inside the silicon and examine its secrets[74], usually shielded by sensors and meshes to detect intrusion.

---

[72] https://lukasstefanko.com/2018/10/android-banking-malware-found-on-google-play-with-over-10000-installs-targets-brazil.html

[73] https://www.apple.com/business/site/docs/iOS_Security_Guide.pdf

[74] https://redmondmag.com/articles/2010/02/03/black-hat-engineer-cracks-tpm-chip.aspx

The FBI was apparently unwilling to go to such lengths in the case of the San Bernardino shooter.

In 2015, a US citizen of Pakistani origin opened fire at a Christmas party in San Bernardino, California, killing 14 and wounding 22. His iPhone was recovered by the FBI, which petitioned Apple to unlock it and discover potential further terrorist plots. After a six-week legal battle, the FBI suddenly withdrew the request, stating that they managed to hack into the iPhone[75], though the theories on how differ. Whether the FBI had access to the phone all along and just wanted to let Apple save face or Apple gave them access but pretended it didn't, or the FBI bought a hacking tool off the black market, we'll never know as the method has been classified.

iPhones can be hacked in other ways, such as by giving them inaudible commands. In DolphinAttack[76], a voice command to dial a number is recorded and played back to an iPhone, which triggers Siri to do as requested. However, when the same voice command is modulated below the human hearing threshold, *and* the iPhone is locked, which should disable Siri, playing back the voice command disengages the lock and makes the iPhone dial the number as if it weren't locked at all.

An interesting implication of this attack is that iPhones are *meant* to have that functionality. When engineers are given a task to produce hardware, they typically look to shave off as much dead weight to simplify the product and stay within budget. Hardware doesn't simply happen to have a certain functionality; if it's there, it was designed like that from the start. We can guess why, but it was probably to – what else – allow ads to have an inaudible layer that can be used to track an individual user or otherwise influence the smartphone.

---

[75] https://www.theguardian.com/technology/2016/mar/28/apple-fbi-case-dropped-san-bernardino-iphone

[76] https://www.youtube.com/watch?v=21HjF4A3WE4

In June 2018, Facebook's research division filed for a patent[77] that would embed inaudible layers in ads and secretly communicate with smartphones. The hidden message would be a series of quick taps, like a Morse code, and would presumably be unique to each ad, ordering the phone to start recording ambient audio such as "the sound of distant human movement and speech". Each ad would, in a sense, be fingerprinted and let Facebook know when, where and how long it was watched to freak users, even more, when they started seeing ads for things they just discussed and saw on TV.

The biggest cybersecurity danger arising from smartphones is the innocuous, persistent tracking done through apps, especially those that deliver ads. Delete all apps you aren't using daily. Do not tolerate ads. On Android, install Block This, a free open-source ad blocker[78]. It's not available on Google Play Store due to violating the Developer Distribution Agreement[79], section 4.9, which states that an app must not disrupt or damage any Google or third-party service; removing or blocking ads embedded in an app falls under this section. On iOS use Adblock Plus[80], though it only blocks ads encountered through Safari and not those loaded by apps.

---

[77] https://metro.co.uk/2018/06/22/facebook-wants-hide-inaudible-messages-tv-ads-force-phone-record-audio-7652112/

[78] https://block-this.com/

[79] https://play.google.com/intl/ALL_us/about/developer-distribution-agreement.html#prohibited

[80] https://itunes.apple.com/app/adblock-plus-abp/id1028871868

Chapter 19 – 2-Factor Authentication (2FA)

Tying up your phone number with your password is an easy way for tech companies to add an extra layer of security with minimal expenses. It's a step in the right direction, but we saw how banks do it: cards are cheap, have a single purpose and are easily replaced. A smartphones is already an attractive target but having 2FA can mean the thief gets a snazzy gadget for free *and* access to your account as a bonus. As more accounts get attached to the same phone, the stakes get exponentially higher, and the phone becomes an Achilles' heel of all those systems rather than an added layer of security.

Enter Mat Honan, Wired.com writer who got hacked in 2012 because he had no 2FA. His heart-rending story[81] is a testament to just how devastating technology can be. Hackers ultimately targeted Mat's Twitter account but started off by calling Apple tech support,

---

[81] https://www.wired.com/2012/08/apple-amazon-mat-honan-hacking/

claiming that they couldn't enter Mat's Me.com email. They couldn't answer any security questions, but they were given a temporary password anyway since they knew Mat's billing address and four digits from his Amazon account card. Here's how.

By researching Mat, hackers found his home address and concluded he probably used it as his billing address. They called up Amazon customer support and asked to add a fake card to the account with his billing address. A few minutes later they called back and asked to add an email address to the account tied to the fake card, which allowed them to reset Mat's Amazon account password and revealed the last four digits of Mat's real card. Using those four digits and the billing address, hackers called Apple customer support to reset Mat's email. From there they reset his Gmail password, entered his Twitter, wiped his iPad and MacBook, deleted his Google account and in just half an hour claimed victory on his Twitter account[82]. The motive for the hack? Mat's Twitter handle has three characters, making it highly sought after. That's it, not trying to influence presidential elections or launch nukes, but plain vanity.

Mat's first mistake was having an email address consisting of only his first and last name. When websites remind you about your email address, they usually show the first and the last character; hackers were smart enough to figure out the rest. When making an email address, vary it up with underscores, numbers or simply misspell your name. Even your name is valuable information; don't make it so that anyone with your email address knows your name.

Mat's second mistake was chaining all his accounts together, which increased the attack surface. Keep your accounts separate from one another and don't fall into the trap of reusing passwords, usernames, addresses, phone numbers, etc. It's a hassle to keep things separate, but in case of a breach, you can count on the rest of your accounts staying safe. As we said at the very start of this book, don't make useless accounts; they increase your attack surface.

---

[82] https://twitter.com/mat/status/231543036159602688

Mat's third mistake was not backing up data. It hurts to have to call customer support and explain your case a hundred times to a hundred different people, but you can avoid the hassle by backing up your data. Buy a USB stick or an external drive and use them solely for backups. Make it a habit to back up everything of value, including browser bookmarks.

Mat's fourth mistake was not using 2FA. Simply attaching a phone number to a login makes it much more difficult to hack. If possible, use an older smartphone and solely for that purpose. This doesn't apply if you're using Facebook.

Facebook uses phone numbers provided for 2FA to help advertisers learn more about users[83]. It's all about ads. When you provide a phone number for 2FA, any advertiser that gets your phone number from other sources can essentially pay to access the hidden advertisement profile Facebook is building on you behind the scenes. What's ironic is that Facebook actually removed the option of *users* searching for people using phone numbers but advertisers can do as they please, as long as they pay.

---

[83] https://www.zdnet.com/article/facebook-is-using-your-2fa-phone-number-to-target-ads-at-you/

Chapter 20 – Quantum Computing

For now, passwords sort of work but the advent of quantum computing might make them completely hackable. When we mentioned a Row Hammering attack, we implied that it exploits the fact tiny components are squeezed together to induce errors. As components get smaller, there's a greater chance they will become unstable, but at some point, there's no making them smaller – we reach a theoretical limit on how small magnetic charge can be and remain stable. So, we might as well find a brand-new paradigm, in this case, quantum computing[84].

The idea is to use sub-atomic particles as components in a computer, making it feasible to create a powerful computer the size of a grain of sand. They will have enormous computing power for a fraction of electricity consumption, making experts worried that they will be used to brute-force encryption keys. We're lucky for now because quantum computers require near absolute zero temperatures, which are possible only in a few labs.

---

[84] https://www.forbes.com/sites/tiriasresearch/2017/10/23/quantum-will-not-break-encryption-yet/#5f87ef547319

Quantum computing will probably not emerge before 2050, and even then, it will be as a proof-of-concept rather than a consumer-ready machine. Until then, our encryption is safe, but quantum computing also promises a new encryption paradigm as quantum states change *if someone observes them*. So, sending a message with a quantum computer means the recipient will know if someone looked at it in transit.

Conclusion

So far, we've seen that the cause of cybersecurity problems isn't code itself as much as its implementation, meaning that it all rests on managers who haven't got the first clue how it all meshes together. They're helped by relatively few programmers who have to account for all kinds of hardware configurations and software environments and ringed by throngs of underpaid support staff reading off of scripts. Security simply can't be maintained by a select few monolithic companies chasing profits. It's all down to us.

We as clever users have to up our standards, choose software built on solid programming practices and support tech companies that are transparent. Even if software is free, we can thank the creator – it really means a lot. We should also look for and deploy customized software solutions that fit our needs rather than use what everyone else is using. In the end, we have to start tinkering with code ourselves, first by writing simple .BAT scripts[85] in any text editor

---

[85] https://www.thetechgame.com/Archives/t=3496964/batch-tutorial-useful-and-cool-batch-scripts.html

and moving onto **Autohotkey** scripts[86] that can automate mouse clicks, register key presses and help us unlock ultimate productivity.

Cybersecurity is by no means a solved problem, and it's likely we'll never find a definite list of actions to take and remain safe in a world filled with electronic devices. What we can do is learn to coexist with them and make sure no hacker can press a button to hijack a smart thermometer and ruin our lives. It doesn't even have to be a checklist as the best cybersecurity practices are simple, lightweight and actually kind of fun. Hackers can't be stopped in a cost-effective way, but they can be made to run around in circles until they give up. Never think you're invincible and be willing to learn from the experts. Banks have shown themselves to have sublime cybersecurity practices, so when in doubt, just ask yourself, "What would my bank do?"

---

[86] https://autohotkey.com/

Glossary

2FA – Two-factor authentication. Attaching a phone number or authenticator to an account.

Admin privilege – Ultimate control of any given system, on par or above of what the owner can do. The Holy Grail of hacking.

Adware – Unwanted program that shows ads. Usually bundled and installed by accident because of banner blindness.

Air gap – Physically separating devices and components from each other or the internet to make them impervious against remote attackers.

Attack vector – Angle from which a hacker attacks some entity.

Attack surface – Exposure to a cyberattack. Complex devices, software bloat, and elaborate usage patterns increase attack surface.

Authenticator – Small physical device producing codes needed to log into a service or account.

Autohotkey – Program for writing standalone textual scripts. Can use any text editor and produce .EXE files.

Backdoor – Alternate access to software or hardware, usually implanted by intelligence agencies.

Banner blindness – Selectively ignoring elements that distract.

Biometric data – Bodily parameters used instead of a password, such as height, fingerprints and face scans.

Bitcoin – Digital fool's gold. Created by Satoshi Nakamoto.

Black hat hacking – Malicious cyber-intrusion. Usually done to disrupt a competitor, wreak havoc or just steal whatever data can be stolen.

Border Gateway Protocol – Code of conduct for internet traffic handlers. Summed up as "be nice to each other".

Botnet – Collection of infected machines used to DoS other targets.

Brendan Eich – Creator of Javascript and co-creator of Firefox.

Bug – Unintended code interaction. If users like a particular bug, it can get promoted to a feature.

Brute force attack – Going through solutions one by one until the right one is found. Hash is meant to make this unfeasible.

Buffer overflow – Erratic behavior of a program when fed data outside its normal data range.

CAPTCHA – Test to distinguish between robots and humans using a website. Commonly presented as "prove you're human". Eventually deprecated in favor of reCAPTCHA.

Catfishing – Pretending to be a sexy female online to drag gullible people into potentially embarrassing and incriminating behavior. Used in social engineering attacks.

Clickbait – Outrageously worded headline to entice clicking on the link and visiting the website. An example would be: "She felt an itch behind her EAR and then the doctors found THIS! DISGUSTING!!!" The actual body of the article may not even reveal what the doctors found.

Closed source – Proprietary software whose code is hidden from the general public.

Compartmentalization – Fragmentation of something for security purposes.

Cookie – Small text file used to identify a user. Initially used for staying logged in but now commonly used for tracking. Origin of the term is from "magic cookie", meaning a small item that makes magic happen.

Cross-site scripting – Injecting third-party malicious code into a website to affect its visitors. Initially referred only to Javascript but now covers all sorts of programming languages.

Cryptojacking – A hacking attack that makes the device mine cryptocurrency in addition to whatever it normally does.

Dictionary attack – Trying to guess a password by going through the list of commonly used words and names: Mary, John, 123456, password, etc.

DolphinAttack – Sending inaudible commands to Siri that overrides any locks.

DoS – Denial of service attack. Aims at disrupting the service to waste time, money and effort.

Duqu – Trojan based off of Stuxnet code. Had independent modules that gave it great flexibility.

Evergreen – Software in a state of constant update. Presented as convenient to the user but meant to disrupt hackers. Promotes feature creep.

Equation Group – Label attached to original creators of Stuxnet, Duqu and Flame.

Feature creep – Constantly upgrading any given piece of software way past its original scope. Increases software bloat and attack surface.

Firewall – Internet traffic filter. Meant to stop unauthorized inbound and outbound traffic.

Firmware – Essential code embedded in the hardware.

Flame – Most complex malware ever found.

Greasemonkey – Add-on for Mozilla Firefox that allows for local code execution in the browser. Google Chrome equivalent is called Tampermonkey.

Hacker – A cyberattacker. Generally uses jury-rigged software and social engineering methods due to low budget.

Hacking – Simple but effective cyberattack. Too expensive and cumbersome to defend against.

Hash – Cryptographic sum of any given data. Meant to produce scrambled (hence, hashed) data that can be used for comparison without exposing it in plaintext.

Hash collision – Finding an alternate hash for any given software or input.

Honeypot – Intentionally vulnerable cyber-target. Meant to analyze hacking attacks and expose hackers.

Identity check – Confirmation of identity. Can be done using something known (password), something owned (authenticator) or some innate quality (biometric data).

Internet of Things – Giving internet connectivity to items that should never have it, such as shoes and umbrellas. Massively increases attack surface.

IP address – Address of a device on any network, including the internet. For example, a home router generally has an IP address 192.168.1.1

Javascript – Dynamic programming language. Can make elements of a webpage adapt to user's actions.

John Draper – A phone phreak that first thought of using a toy whistle.

Kernel – Computer core. Fastest performance. Reserved for the most essential functions in a computer.

Kevin Mitnick – The most notorious hacker ever. Now runs a security firm and gets paid for doing what once landed him in jail.

Keylogger – Program that covertly records and transmits keystrokes.

Machine learning – A broad concept of creating a machine that can update its own software.

Metadata – Impersonal data, such as how many times users clicked the left mouse button while visiting a website, but not which website they visited. Harmless in single instances but intrusive when aggregated.

Mitigation defense – Software philosophy that doesn't try to stop hacking but simply mitigate its effects.

Mt. Gox – Defunct Bitcoin exchange. Hacked in 2014.

NSA – Most commonly blamed US agency when it comes to digital surveillance.

Open source – Software whose code is free to use, share and modify. The ideal kind of software.

Password – Unique phrase that allows access.

Peter Principle – Idea that employees fail upwards. "Cream rises until it sours". Explains why companies lose their touch with reality and become susceptible to hacking.

Phishing – Misrepresentation of links, websites, and services to make the user reveal private data.

Phone phreaks – Landline network hackers during the 1960s. Used toy whistles to mimic modems communicating with one another.

Piggyback programs – Programs bundled with what the user downloaded in the hope that he or she simply press "Next" by habit and installs them.

Plaintext – Human-readable text, like the one in this book. Insecure but accessible.

Plugins – Custom additions to software, giving it extra functionality.

PRISM – Comprehensive NSA spying program. Consists of complete admin access to servers of tech companies, such as Google, Facebook, and others.

Private data – Personally identifiable data, such as name, address, phone number, etc., or data that gives admin privilege.

Ransomware – Malware that encrypts files and deletes them if no ransom is paid.

ReCAPTCHA – Upgraded CAPTCHA challenge. Asks the user to identify objects from minute, grainy images.

Rootkit – Malware that hijacks administrator privileges on a machine to conceal itself.

Row Hammering – Vibrating components in a RAM stick so quickly that it reprograms nearby components with malware. Jumps the air gap.

Salt – Minute addition to a hash to reduce hash collision.

Sandboxing – Isolating processes or browser tabs from one another and the rest of the computer. Increases security but affects performance.

Script kiddies – Inexperienced and immature hackers who rely completely on automated scripts and malware.

Script – The simplest form of software, meant to do one thing quickly and efficiently. Can even be written in word editors such as Notepad.

Security through obscurity – Hiding the real functions and purpose of software from the user, supposedly to thwart hackers.

Six principles of persuasion – Dr. Robert Cialdini's theory on how to manipulate people into doing what we want. Typically used in social engineering attacks but also by telemarketers, fundraisers, etc.

Social engineering – Exploiting inherent human trust to gain access to private data. As easy as dialing a number and politely asking.

Software bloat – Tendency of software to become bigger, slower and less efficient as time goes on. The governing rule is that it's easy to add features but almost impossible to remove them.

Spoofing – Changing one's own originating information to impersonate an identity and gain the trust of someone else.

Spyware – Spying program that scoops up private data or metadata.

Stuxnet – Virus that specifically targeted Iranian uranium enrichment facilities.

Technobabble – Gibberish that sounds like genuine technical jargon. Meant to impress and move the story along but falls apart under closer scrutiny.

Third party content – Mishmash of content served to users by websites they have no idea of. May have had beneficial uses at first but now comprehensively abused.

Trialware – Intrusive software that promises utility but locks up and asks for payment shortly afterward.

Trojan – Malware that opens a backdoor in the infected machine for a hacker.

Turing test – Set of standards that means an artificial intelligence can pass off as human.

Turla – Hacker groups infiltrating political, governmental entities and stealing information over the course of years. Possibly state-sponsored.

Virus – Malware meant to incapacitate a machine.

White hat hacking – Cyber-intrusion meant to do minimal damage. Usually done out of curiosity.

Worm – Malware meant to replicate as fast as possible. Generally spreads through email.

Yippies – Members of the Youth International Party in the 1960s. Best described as terrorist hippies.

Zero-day exploit – Previously unknown and unpatched bug or backdoor in software. Fetches a substantial price on the black market.

Zusy – Worm spread through Facebook.

Made in the USA
Monee, IL
03 August 2022

10833524R00069